Navigating
the
Mortgage
Maze

An Interactive, High-Tech Guide
to Financing Your Home

Andrew E. Turnauer, Jr.

AN OWL BOOK

HENRY HOLT AND COMPANY

NEW YORK

Henry Holt and Company, Inc.
Publishers since 1866
115 West 18th Street
New York, New York 10011

Henry Holt® is a registered
trademark of Henry Holt and Company, Inc.

Library of Congress Cataloging-in-Publication Data
Turnauer, Jr., Andrew E.
Navigating the mortgage maze :
an interactive, high-tech guide to financing your home /
Andrew E. Turnauer, Jr.—1st ed.
p.   cm.
1. Mortgage loans—United States.
2. Mortgage loans—United States—Computer network resources.
3. Mortgage loans—United States—Software.
I. QualifyR II. Title.

H32040.5.U5T87 1996	96-28665
332.7′22—dc20	CIP

ISBN 0-8050-4773-5

Henry Holt books are available for special
promotions and premiums. For details contact:
Director, Special Markets.

First Edition—1996

Design, development and production:
Jennings & Keefe, Inc.
Corte Madera, CA

Printed in the United States of America
All first editions are printed on acid-free paper. ∞
1   3   5   7   9   10   8   6   4   2

Dedication

I dedicate this book to Donna, my wife of 19 years, and my children Lauren and Andrew, and to Dr. Mark Singer. You all helped me navigate through the "Cancer Maze" during which this book was conceived. Then you helped me turn the conception into a reality. God bless you and thank you.

Acknowledgments

The tireless dedication of a number of very special people made this book possible. Maryann Karinch turned my ideas and words into concepts and complete sentences. Betty Rogers, my mother-in-law, and Marge Turnauer, my mom, proofread, reproofed, and proofread again.

Cindy Jennings added special touches with editing and encouragement. Jeff Gates, author of the QualifyR software program, allowed a version of his program to be part of this integrated book/software package. Jennings and Keefe guided the project through the publishing labyrinth.

And "mega" thanks go to my partner Brenda Cantu and my staff Imran Mahmood, Marsha Lancaster, and Rachel Wight who kept the office running, loans funding, and the underwriters at bay while I played writer.

Contents

Introduction

The word "mortgage" has its roots in Latin. "Mort" + "gage" means, essentially, "a pledge until death." Some borrowers might say signing a mortgage connotes, "A pledge to die," depending on how exasperating the process is or how high their final loan payments are.

Steering through the convoluted Mortgage Maze is similar for everyone. The one issue that binds the majority of borrowers is the lender's continual request for documentation. Someone constantly demands information that seems redundant or obvious.

Since it's next to impossible for people outside the real estate industry to anticipate each requirement, the mortgage process takes on the appearance of a maze. By the time most people get their loan, they are dizzy and exhausted from trying to get through it.

This book won't transform the crooked maze into a straight stretch of highway, but it will alert you to the abrupt turns and bumpy pieces of road so your journey will be less stressful.

TRUE STORIES—NAMES CHANGED TO PROTECT THE BORROWERS

Yes, it can happen to you. But you aren't alone. People, every day, everywhere encounter the same challenges and emotional trauma that you could encounter during your path through the mortgage maze. Situations as complex or simple as name changes due to marriage or divorce, a quick career climb to the top by moving six times in four years, saying yes to too many low-cost credit card solicitations, always paying cash, and accepting money from your parents for a down payment can put a quick stop sign in the path of the lender. The True Story sections of this book will give you confidence to proceed with the vision to anticipate the curvy road in your personal mortgage maze.

USING YOUR COMPUTER TO MAKE THE RIGHT CHOICES

The QualifyR software included with this book represents one of the most unique aspects of Navigating the Mortgage Maze. It is derived from a software program developed by Jeff Gates and modified for your use with this book. QualifyR will let you play "If . . . then" with the mortgage prequalification process. You can compare the effect of any type of loan on your financial position.

Additional help is available at the Web site www.maze.com. This site was developed by the author and Brenda Cantu. Maze.com gives you easy access to all the components of purchasing or refinancing a home. You can get your own credit report, including credit scoring (not available to consumers directly from credit bureaus), home value information about your current or desired property, as well as apply for a loan, secure pre-approval, and open your own escrow account.

When you use these resources before you contact a mortgage professional, you will already know the most important questions to ask, how you fit into their ratios, how much money you will need for a down payment, how much house you can afford, and many of the other requirements which would be mysterious and stressful without your computer's help. It is possible that you will encounter no surprises on your trip. Most importantly you can learn where your "borrowing" strengths are and when to use them to your advantage. The house of your dreams will be yours at the loan terms and cost you want.

MASTERING MORTGAGE JARGON

Every profession develops its own jargon. Since you probably apply infrequently for a mortgage, even the applications can be confusing. To say nothing of the first visit with a "bad lender" who talks to you about a full doc, FIRM, balloon, ARM, quick qualifier, or neg am without explaining one word. This book is designed to introduce the language of the mortgage industry. The first time a mortgage term is used, it is italicized. This means it is not only fully discussed in the text, but also defined again in the glossary and indexed at the end of the book.

MAPPING THE MORTGAGE MAZE

Clearly the process of applying for a mortgage approaches the stress and complication of filing annual income tax forms. This book will navigate you through the mortgage maze by presenting the concepts you need to understand the process and by telling stories to highlight specific problems and their solutions. When you understand who loans money, why, what they want to see from you and when, and the rules they usually play by, you can control your mortgage destiny.

Navigating the Mortgage Maze makes it easy to browse the table of contents, the glossary, the index, and the book to focus on what you need to know. We have devised a visual system of icons to identify certain situations which you will quickly begin to recognize.

Avoid Common Problems! The detour sign alerts you to common problems occurring during the mortgage process. This hint will give you information on how to avoid them. For example, avoiding differences between debt and payment schedules on your credit report and application or avoiding a problem with a no income mortgage application by paying a few bucks for the required business license you never got. Another common problem to avoid is the dead bug syndrome—your 1975 VW bug is dying, but you ignore the impending burden of new payments in assessing your ability to handle a mortgage. Don't do it!

Manage Difficult Circumstances! In the mortgage maze, you can proceed with caution down the curviest roads if you understand what the mortgage professionals need to know and how they look at the specific information you provide. The caution sign will alert you to situations you need to manage before the mortgagor manages them for you like the fact that your credit record reflects late payments every August when you're on vacation. Or managing the lender who suspects the $30,000 in your bank account is ill-gotten gains because it is more than your annual salary. Or assuring that the IRS form 4506 specifies only the tax return years needed by the lender, instead of giving the lender unlimited access.

 Drive by the Rules! The driving rules of the Mortgage Maze exist just like rules of the road in a driving manual. This drivers manual symbol alerts you to some of the rules of the mortgage maze such as perfect documentation necessary when including income from a second job, using the advantages created by the Fair Credit Reporting Act, disputing a lien on your credit report, and supplying acceptable documentation for a passive income source.

 Package the Application Perfectly! How you present yourself to the mortgage professional can make the difference between yes and no, higher or lower interest rates, and favorable or unfavorable terms. A good example would be the fact that your union contract guarantees yearly cost-of-living increases. Tell that to the lender on your application. This book will tell you how to gift wrap your loan application to achieve your mortgage goals.

 Compute to Win! The computer symbol alerts you to go to your computer for certain mortgage decision-making. Whoever loans you money for your home will be using computers to determine how credit-worthy you are, whether you meet their criteria, and how much and under what terms they should loan money to you. You can use the QualifyR software and Internet Web sites to anticipate how they will see you on their screen.

Maze Master Opinions! These include information that comes from years of experience in the mortgage industry working with people to secure loans and people who loan money to them. Steering through the mortgage maze can be easier if you are familiar with some of the concepts and ideas that aren't in the rule books, guidelines, or on the applications. The Maze Master Opinions can open doors that appear closed.

INSTALLING QUALIFYR

QualifyR is written in Visual Basic 3.0, a Microsoft programming language. The program will run on IBM/PC computers (286 to 486 and Pentium Processors) running Windows 3.1 and Windows 95.

To install QualifyR, double-click on SETUP.EXE and you will be asked where you want the application installed, for example, C:/QUALIFYR. Then proceed.

If you receive an error message,

1. Exit Windows.

2. Turn the computer off.

3. Turn the computer on.

4. Run SETUP.EXE as the first Windows activity.

If you are one of the very few people who has an installation problem after this, please read the file called _PROBLEM.TXT, which addresses specific error messages.

Chapter 1

An Aerial View
of the Mortgage Maze

There is a mortgage package for virtually everyone. An aerial view of the Mortgage Maze explains the process so that even if you're a square peg, you will find a square hole where you fit comfortably.

THE STRAIGHT ROAD TO HOME OWNERSHIP

Imagine a world where everyone pays bills on time and saves ten percent of all wages. In that fantastic world, buying a home would be a simple five-step process.

1. Figure out how much you can afford (prequalifying).

2. Search for a desirable house in your price range.

3. Apply for a loan.

4. Negotiate with the lender and the property owner to get the best prices and terms.

5. Close the deal.

Even though the path to home-buying in this world of twisted and complex financial arrangements is a maze, it is shaped by that same five-step process. This book will get you from one step to the next efficiently. It will help you take the straightest path possible.

Does Everyone Go Through This?

John Turner wanted a mortgage. With a one million dollar trust fund and a steady job as Executive Director of a community service organization, he assumed "No problem." Then John discovered the Mortgage Maze—a twisted road from desire for a house to home ownership.

If you've ever been turned down for a mortgage or had difficulty getting one, you know what John faced. And you can join the crowd. The Mortgage Maze has abrupt turns, bumps, deadends, and tolls. Yet, for many people, ownership makes a house a home. So the trek has a grand purpose and great rewards.

Years ago, lenders used common sense as their main criterion for loan qualification; personal knowledge of wages and honorable qualities meant instant success. Conversely, personal knowledge of a terminal illness or family scandal could have meant instant failure. Now, the lender's decision is based on an objective system of rating and grading in which the "four C's"—credit, collateral, capacity, and character—have become the "three-and-a-half C's." In other words, your assets and liabilities affect your borrowing status far more than the qualitative assessment of your stability or character. And the numbers that were guidelines for a local banker on the loan application are now standards for acceptance or rejection.

Categorically, the loan process has grown less and less personal. There is computerized *underwriting, credit scoring*, and *appraisal*—all done in an instant. And the most frustrating part is that so much weight is given to a snapshot of your finances today. If you don't fulfill the lender's requirements at this moment, your application is spit out of the system. So, if the rules say that John Turner is a high-risk borrower because he has all his money in one bank, he may have a few more turns and obstacles to steer around before he gets out of the Mortgage Maze.

Why the shift in the mortgage process to such severe objectivity? In brief, some lenders were mortgage-rich. They had too many loans with the associated risks and interest income. Others were mortgage-poor. For example, a bank in California might have originated lots of mortgages, while one in the Midwest might have done only a handful for farm properties. It became evident that if a heavily committed bank could "sell" mortgages to another one, then the first bank would have more money for additional loans and the second would have a heftier portfolio of them, creating a higher *return on assets* (ROA). In general, *selling a mortgage* means the lender gets the amount of the loan, but transfers the risk and interest-earning potential to another lender.

Initially, the transfer involved a couple of bankers getting together with their cigars and a portfolio to set parameters. The buying banker might say, "I'll take all the purchase money loans made with a 20 percent or higher down payment." Then, before signing an agreement, the two bankers would drive past the properties to inspect the collateral.

In 1984, Farmer's Savings Bank used this kind of transaction as the basis for a business scheme that revolutionized the way home loans moved from the originating source, that is, from the *primary market* to the *secondary market*. Teams of Farmer's underwriters flew all over the country, inspecting property, underwriting, and buying loans. By 1985, this little bank based just outside of Sacramento, California had amassed huge mortgage portfolios, and had become the largest seller of loans to the *Federal National Mortgage Association*, called *Fannie Mae*.

Fannie Mae, which is federally chartered but shareholder-owned, has a mission to provide financial products and services that make it more affordable for Americans to own homes. It does this through the secondary mortgage market by buying mortgages from banks to replenish their cash for more mortgages—the same principle the mortgage-rich and mortgage-poor banks used to strengthen their positions. The fact that Fannie Mae, like a lot of banks, is shareholder-owned is critical to understanding what happened next.

The success of Farmer's Bank, short-lived as it was, fired up the secondary mortgage business so much that more banks wanted a piece of the action. Fannie Mae knew that in order for the secondary market to continue to be efficient and reliable, lending guidelines had to be more tightly and automatically enforced. The alternative meant putting its investors at risk.

In short, the current exacting mortgage process reflects the lending institution's need to protect its investors. In time and dollars, borrowers pay the cost of protecting the secondary mortgage market.

What does this mean for you? First, your mortgage lender has no face and no personality when it comes to making judgments about your credit, collateral, and capacity. You don't have to worry about offending him or her, because your lender is an "it" in dealing with dollars and percentages. You won't be any more persuasive if you try to color the truth about your finances. Second, your mortgage lender has a face and personality when it comes to making judgments about your character. When the subjective aspects of your loan application come into play, you must confront either the opportunity or the frustration of dealing with someone whose opinion of your stability counts. Third, even though the mortgage process is, by nature, convoluted, it is possible to move straight through it.

Keep these thoughts in mind as we enter the Mortgage Maze and show you how to get from desire to home ownership.

HOW DO YOU PICK A HOUSE THAT WILL BE A HOME?

This book focuses on the financial aspects of buying a home, that is, Steps 1, 3, 4, and 5 which include prequalifying, applying for a loan, negotiating, and closing. Nevertheless, since there are numerous references to *collateral* throughout the text, it is important to address Step 2, selecting a property.

To launch the discussion, here is a bit of heresy:

In the Maze Master's opinion . . .
A single-family, owner-occupied home is not an investment.
It is your home—a roof over your head.

Don't begin the mortgage process with illusions that dramatic *appreciation* of your house will make up for any belt-tightening you did to get it. Select your property using logical criteria.

One most logical criterion is to buy a house that is more likely to *appreciate* than *depreciate*. This subject is a whole book in itself. However, if you buy the least expensive house in a desirable neighborhood and add value through improvements, you are more likely to see financial gains than if you buy the best house in the same neighborhood. The increase in value through *sweat equity* is the only guaranteed gain possible in a flat market.

THE NEIGHBORHOOD

"Where can I afford to live?" is the first question you must ask. After you have a general idea, do a needs assessment that points to appropriate neighborhoods for you. Then drive through selected areas at various times of the day and days of the week. Seek answers to questions about proximity to certain things, as well as features of the property itself. Is the neighborhood close to the people and activities you care about? Or is it too close to things you want to stay away from! Some aspects of the issues to address might include the following: friends, in-laws, work, school, shopping, gym, church, highway, trains, and planes.

In assessing the features of the neighborhood, it is helpful to have a real estate agent who knows the area. "For sale" signs in the area, as well as a few phone calls, should quickly reveal which realty company handles the bulk of transactions in your target neighborhood. Get a full-time agent who is currently working on sales in that area and find out something about the people, the pets, and the parties on Saturday night. Find out everything that's important to you through the agent and also from looking around. Among the features you might consider are parking for guests, traffic flow and noise, a neighborhood watch, street lighting, placement of fire hydrants or power lines, drainage patterns, sewer system, and water supply.

THE PROPERTY

Next, do a needs assessment that ensures that you have sound reasons for liking a particular property. According to most real estate agents and *mortgage brokers*, somewhere between 5 and 15 percent of home buys are on impulse. In other words, there are a lot of hard-working people out there who become so enamored with a Jacuzzi in the master bathroom or a spectacular view that they sink their life's savings into the wrong house!

TRUE STORY: BUYING THE WRONG HOUSE

Jane and Joe Greene decided to transplant their graphic arts business from Los Angeles to Chicago. While looking for a place near the city, Joe discovered a beautiful suburb. After visiting once, without their two children, Jane agreed with Joe that the neighborhood was ideal—close to schools, recreational facilities, and an on-ramp to the highway leading into the city. In June, they moved into a house with a panoramic view of a lake. They moved out as soon as the next school year was over.

Jane and Joe never considered their daily lifestyle when they bought the house with the view. Dreaming only of weekend hikes with the kids, and afternoons on a boat, they never weighed the importance of walking and driving up and down a steep, winding, and sometimes icy, hill to their house a dozen times a day. One winter was all they could take of their dream house before their knees and humor wore out.

The needs assessment involves questions about your future, as well as your current schedule and lifestyle. If, within the next five years, you anticipate dramatic shifts in either, consider how the property will accommodate you.

- Will you have more children, or, will your children be going from a nearby daycare center to a school ten miles away?

- Is your health steady? Would stairs be a blessing or a trauma for you?

- Maybe your mother's health is failing, and you need to be prepared to bring her to your home. If she is in a wheelchair, will the house allow easy access and mobility from room to room?

- Will you ever work at home?

- Does the house allow for the level of privacy you want?

When you are forced to make a change in residence because of circumstances that are somewhat predictable—like a pregnancy or extended visits from a parent—you face deadlines and pressure that might have been avoided.

WHO SHOULD BE ON YOUR TEAM?

Did you notice that I recommended getting a "full-time real estate agent" earlier in the chapter? Here is another recommendation: choose a full-time mortgage broker. The mortgage broker is a person who will represent you to the lender for the purchase of the home and the origination of the mortgage. In selecting a broker, who earns a fee for processing your loan documents and guiding you toward the best loan for your situation, you want to keep two statistics in mind: Eighty percent of the real estate transactions are handled by 20 percent of the professionals, and 20 percent of that elite group completes most of the transactions. The field is littered with part-timers who do not have the skills or knowledge to bring many deals to closure. You do not want them on your team. You do want the top 20 percent of the elite, the 20 percent who know the following:

- Property values in and characteristics of the neighborhoods they "work";

- The consistency of different lenders in their calculation of *annual percentage rate (APR)* and loan processing;

- How to skillfully match the type of mortgage to the buyer;

- Industry trends; and

- Reliable title and escrow companies, appraisers, and inspectors.

When you're ready to do business, find these people through your real estate agent or experienced home buyers and ask them tough questions about their fees. Case studies and tips throughout the book will point to other issues that you will want to address with prospective agents, brokers and lenders, as well as guidelines on evaluating their responses. The one quality all members of your team must have, no matter what their answers, is that of good listening.

Understand everything fully up front. You have a right to know every detail, so ask for explanations. If you feel like the fog is rolling in because your agent or broker responds in mortgage jargon, say, "Put it in plain talk, please," followed by, "Put it in plain talk, or else" if that doesn't get the desired result.

You are about to make the biggest, or one of the biggest, purchases of your life. The amount you spend should be comfortable for you, the place you select should meet all your major needs, and the people with whom you do business should pay attention to what you say. These principles are fundamental to getting through the Mortgage Maze with ease.

Chapter 2

A Strong Start:
Look Good on Paper

A strong start through the Mortgage Maze means looking good on paper to the lender. Certain critical financial information will affect your ability to get a loan. You will discover what data goes in, what stays out, and how to substantiate the facts and figures that lenders use to determine if you qualify for a loan. This chapter guides you through the QualifyR software exercises that help you gain real control over the qualifying process. QualifyR makes it easy to run a self-evaluation using a wide range of variables that fit your personal situation. You will know what you can afford, even if lenders say otherwise.

WHY SELF-QUALIFY?

The actions taken by Fannie Mae and its secondary marketing businesses to protect their investors have since sent lenders and borrowers into shock. As of 1995, Fannie Mae's brother, *Freddie Mac* (Federal Home Loan Mortgage Corporation) disapproved nearly half of all loans already underwritten when it subjected them to the scrutiny of a computerized loan-origination system. That means that either or all of three underwriting sources—a lender, a broker and a mortgage insurance underwriter—missed red flags in half the loan packages they approved. The rejected borrowers who still wanted a mortgage, had to struggle through the loan process again to accommodate Freddie Mac's computers in Washington, D.C.

You can do a lot to avert this detour. A *self-qualification*, or a self-assessment of your income and debt, will help you collect, examine and weigh all the financial facts that determine your borrowing status.

PREQUALIFICATION OR PRE-DISQUALIFICATION?

Many people think they can accomplish self-qualification by going through a *prequalification* process with a lender. Consider the loan professional who takes a prospective borrower through prequalification. They are trained and paid to think systematically. Paradoxically, that same systematic approach often misses critical information and gives you a distorted view of your borrowing power.

Filling out blocks and blanks sequentially is a systematic effort. Your ability to buy a home, however, is the information in those blocks and blanks combined together. If you self-qualify prior to exposing yourself to the lender's forms, you can construct an accurate picture of yourself as a borrower. You'll know what the loan application *should* say about you, so you'll be keenly aware of how the data in the different blocks and blanks reinforce or detract from your position. Later, if a lender disagrees with your self-assessment, you have a right to suspect that the lender or the lender's computer is wrong.

Real estate and loan professionals are also trained to think realistically. Part of their job is keep your eyes trained on the obstacles in the Mortgage Maze. If you're aiming for a dream house, the first leg of your trip should be one that puts your eyes on the vista, not the obstacles. You want a high-ground view of all the possibilities. You don't want someone to put blinders on you, then watch you stumble down a rocky road.

In the Maze Master's opinion . . .
If you ask better questions of yourself than the mortgage
pros ask, you'll get better answers.

The prequalification process sounds like a shortcut to the word "yes" from a lender. "It'll just take five minutes, ma'am!" says the financial services officer at the local bank. In fact, it might be more appropriately called a pre disqualification process, and it could be a big pothole that throws you off balance right after you put yourself into a confident frame of mind about entering the Mortgage Maze.

Here are the questions asked on a typical prequalification form, along with the hidden meaning behind the question:

- What is your social security number? This means that the bank needs it to run a quick credit check.

- What is your zip code? This indicates whether you might qualify for a *Community Reinvestment Act* loan or other loan which is a relatively low-interest rate loan for a low-income community.

- What is your annual household income? If it is below a certain level, you could qualify for a special program. Then again, if it is too low below a certain level, the lender may not want to deal with you.

- What are your monthly debt payments? This excludes current mortgage, if you are selling your house, or rental payments.

- How much cash will you have after closing? Most lenders want to see *cash reserves* of at least three months of the estimated principle plus interest plus taxes plus insurance, or *PITI*, and *homeowners dues* if you are going to live in a *condominium*.

- What type of mortgage are you interested in? *Fixed* and *Adjustable Rate Mortgage* (ARM) are the two main types, and what the lender expects to see on the form at this stage.

- How long at your current address? This question, and the following two, theoretically give a sense of your stability. In fact, this is often not the case.

- How long at previous address?

- How long at current job?

- What percent down payment will you make? The question is really, "How much do you want us to give you?"

Based on your answers, the lender's computer draws a rough sketch of you as a borrower. It's like having an artist draw a picture of you after hearing over the telephone, "I'm six feet tall, 45 years old and weigh 170 pounds."

There are also financial distinctions that distinguish you from other people in your zip code or from people who earn the same annual salary as you. They won't surface in prequalification and they may not surface in a routine qualification procedure. Unfortunately, misunderstandings may be the only things that surface if the potential borrower is not aware of how to go beyond the form.

Two different lending institutions can easily appraise you financially as two different people.

A VISIT WITH A BAD LENDER

Harriet Blackwell is beginning her first meeting with a loan officer at Big City Bank. Although this scenario has Big City Bank represented by a person, if Harriet were to fill out a prequalification form without ever talking with anyone, the result would be the same. There wouldn't be any conversation involved.

BCB Loan Officer:	"Let's start with your monthly income."
Harriet:	"$2,500."
BCB Loan Officer:	"And what do you think your monthly debt is?"
Harriet:	"$1,500."
BCB Loan Officer:	"My, that's high. How's your credit?"
Harriet:	"It's mostly good, I guess. I have been late on some credit card payments."
BCB Loan Officer:	"How late?"
Harriet:	"About 30 days."
BCB Loan Officer:	"This could be derogatory credit. How much cash do you have in the bank?"
Harriet:	"I have $23,000 saved up for a down payment."
BCB Loan Officer:	"Very good. I suppose you're looking at a condo for $80,000 or $90,000, right?"
Harriet:	"Actually, no. I have my heart set on a two-bedroom house so my daughter can have her own room. It lists for $150,000."
BCB Loan Officer:	"My, oh, my. I'm afraid there's nothing we can do for you. But thanks for thinking of Big City Bank."

A VISIT WITH A GOOD LENDER

Bitter and confused, Harriet reluctantly keeps her other appointment for a prequalification at Second Big City Bank. This time, a thinking human being is available to ensure that Harriet knows how to fill in the blanks. A clearly written form should have the same effect.

SBCB Loan Officer:	"Let's start with your monthly income."
Harriet:	"$2,500."
SBCB Loan Officer:	"Is that before or after taxes?"
Harriet:	"After."
SBCB Loan Officer:	"Fortunately, lenders look at gross income."
Harriet:	"Then, let's see. I make $40,000 a year. So it's about $3,300."
SBCB Loan Officer:	"And what do you think your monthly debt is?"
Harriet:	"$1,500."
SBCB Loan Officer:	"My, that's high. Does that include rent?"
Harriet:	"Yes. $750."
SBCB Loan Officer:	"Okay, we can take that out. So, we're looking at $750. How's your credit?"
Harriet:	"I thought it was good, but the other banker said it was derogatory because I've been late on some credit card payments."
SBCB Loan Officer:	"How late?"
Harriet:	"About 30 days."
SBCB Loan Officer:	"Did this happen a lot?"
Harriet:	"No, just about six months. I got behind when my daughter was sick."
SBCB Loan Officer:	"That doesn't sound like derogatory credit to me. How much cash do you have in the bank?"
Harriet:	"I have $23,000 saved up for a down payment."
SBCB Loan Officer:	"Very good. Now all we have to do is match your dollars to your dreams."

The good lender started to help Harriet compose a more accurate picture of her borrowing status, but many of the positives still never showed up because Harriet did not know how to introduce other distinctions into the evaluation process. She was still at the mercy and lack of imagination of the lender.

A self-qualifying exercise helps you ascertain what those distinctions are; it helps you ask better questions. It stimulates your thinking about what you really bring to the table and reflects what you want to spend. A lender guiding you through the qualification process will naturally be far more interested in quantifying what you can spend, rather than justifying what you want to spend, no matter how diligent and cooperative that person may be.

In preparing to self-qualify, you can turn to the QualifyR software included with this book, or use the calculators at a number of Websites, such as www.maze.com. Using the software is an easy way to become familiar with the variables in a qualification process. Think of the book and software samples as even more helpful versions of the good lender in the sketch above.

THE PROCESS OF SELF-QUALIFYING

The first action to self-qualification is income assessment. Therefore, if you begin with the *Residential Loan Application* (also called Fannie Mae Form 1003 or Freddie Mac Form 65), rather than the QualifyR calculation software, ignore the first four sections. Sections I–IV are not self-explanatory, and Chapter 6 guides you through these sections of the loan application in great detail. The Residential Loan Application is available in full at www.maze.com.

 Let's say Harriet opts to take control of her mortgage process. Despite her learning experience with the two loan officers, she still does not know what questions to ask a real estate professional about qualifying for a loan. She still doesn't know what she doesn't know. She decides to use the QualifyR software to analyze her income and debt situation.

INCOME

Harriet may earn $40,000 a year as an x-ray technician, but her income can also include other money. Here is how the QualifyR software, relying on information from Harriet's tax return, helped her examine other income.

Income Analysis		Monthly Average: $4,004			
A Personal Income, Form 1010			1994	1995	1996
1.	Adjusted Gross Income	+	38750	40500	42750
2.	Other Income	–	0	0	0
3.	Tax-Exempt Interest Income	+	140	188	202
4.	State Tax Refund	–	0	0	0
5.	Alimony Received (Nonrecurring)	–	0	0	0
6.	Nontaxable Pensions, Annuities	+	0	0	0
7.	Nonrecurring Unemployment Compensation	–	0	0	0
8.	Nontaxable Social Security	+	0	0	0
9.	Non Self-Employed Wages	–	0	0	0
10.	Child Support Received (Recurring)	+	7200	7200	7200
11.	IRA / Keogh Contributions	+	0	0	0
12.	Self-Employed Health Insurance Deduction	+	0	0	0
13.	Alimony Paid (And Deducted on 1040)	+	0	0	0
	Allowable Income Per Year		46090	47888	50152

This checklist can serve as a companion to the software form. Keep in mind that a lender looks at gross, not net, figures.

- Wages from another job
- Overtime
- Bonus
- Child support
- Alimony
- Maintenance payments
- Rental property income
- Interest and dividends
- Trailing Spouse Income
- Trust income
- Retirement income
- Social security
- Notes receivable
- Veterans benefits
- Unemployment and welfare benefits
- Auto allowance

There are conditions related to some of the income sources. Most have to do with how long and/or how consistently the income is received.

If you have a *second job*, you must be able to document that it is continuing employment, not just a short-term exercise to improve your cash flow this month. A less objective criterion is that the second job should have a relationship to the first, although that is not as important as the job continuing. Second job examples would include a police officer moonlighting as a security guard or a teacher who works weekends as a librarian.

Here are stories that illustrate conditions for other income acceptability.

TRUE STORY: AUTO ALLOWANCE ACCEPTED

The computer company for which Henry Newman was a sales representative laid him off, but continued all benefits for a two-month period after his termination. This included an auto allowance. In the meantime, Henry got another job as a rep for a competing company, which also provided an auto allowance.

Even though he changed jobs, his supplemental income in the form of an auto allowance continued uninterrupted and could be verified for the minimum 24-month period. His proof was that it appeared on Internal Revenue Service (IRS) form 2106.

The way Henry's lender accepted the auto allowance was by removing the monthly car payment from his debt. The allowance, therefore, did not add to Henry's income, it reduced his debt.

TRUE STORY: CHILD SUPPORT UNDERSTATED

Naomi Evern's two boys are in private school, and her former husband committed to pay their tuition. In theory, she is supposed to receive $1,500 a month for tuition and living expenses. In reality, her former husband has not paid more than $800 a month for over a year, so she cannot verify a higher level of child support for the previous 12-month period. Will Naomi have to submit verification of income OR will she "get away with" providing the decree that states the amount she is supposed to receive? Lender's choice!

Of course, the lender won't care what Naomi is supposed to receive if she's late with a mortgage payment.

TRUE STORY: RENTAL INCOME REDUCED

When Maryann Garner moved to Arizona, she decided to rent her house in Ohio. She was surprised to learn that her "rental income" did not positively affect her ability to buy a new home. It affected it negatively! For purposes of qualifying for a mortgage, rental income is calculated as follows:

Gross Rental
- 25%
- The Monthly Mortgage Payment (PITI)
Net Rental Income

Since Maryann only rented her house for the same amount as the mortgage, she could not show positive cash flow on the arrangement. Moreover, on paper it looked like a loss.

TRUE STORY: CONSISTENT UNEMPLOYMENT BENEFITS

Wayne Barns is a member of Actor's Equity, the union for legitimate theater professionals. Every year since college he has worked "summer stock" in New York's Catskill Mountains, but his employment in the theater from October to April has not been regular. He receives unemployment benefits when he does not have an acting job. His work might be termed "seasonal," but his year-long income picture does have a pattern. There is consistency in his finances, and he can prove it through records from the past 24 months.

Three important questions to ask a professional if you have doubts about your income are, "Does this source count as income?" "How long must I receive this income for it to count?" and "What do I need to verify it?"

DEBT

Total monthly obligations or debt can also be a longer list than you might think. For example, if you pay for your own health insurance and have every intention of maintaining it, then it is a monthly obligation that affects your ability to pay off a mortgage.

Some people go too far, though, in confessing their debt. If you run up a credit card bill of $1,500 every month because you use it as a convenience at the grocery store, dry cleaner and so on, then pay it off every month, you don't add a penny to your consumer debt. Because you pay it off, its effect on your total monthly obligations is $0.

Harriet went to the debt module of the QualifyR software to make a list of her obligations.

Monthly Debt Item / Account No.	Monthly Pmt.	Monthly Debt Item / Account No.	Monthly Pmt.
car payment	250		0
VISA Card Payment	300		0
Pre-school	200		0
	0		0
	0		0
	0		0
	0		0
	0		0
	0		0
	0		0
	0		0
	0		0
	0		0
	0		0
	0	Total Monthly Debt / All Items	750

Debt payments are divided into two types: *installment debt* and *revolving debt*. On installment debts, such as a car loan, you pay the same amount every month for the life of the loan. Harriet's monthly payments of $200 to the pre-school her daughter attends also fall into this category, since the tuition is billed at $2,400 annually.

Debts of less than ten months do not count when it comes to qualifying for a mortgage. Do not include them in your debt profile.

On revolving debts, such as credit cards, you are required to pay a portion of the balance each month. In calculating your debt, a lender usually considers your monthly obligation five percent of your balance, whereas your creditor may require a greater or lesser amount

If you hold credit cards that require less than 5 percent of the balance as a monthly payment, use this statement as documentation that your monthly debt is lower than the default calculation. In other words, if your debt related to revolving charges is $3,000, a lender would automatically calculate that your monthly obligation is $150, or 5 percent. If the $3,000 represents debt related to a department store charge account and a VISA account that only require 3 percent/month on the balance, however, your cash position improves by $90/month. That means thousands in added buying power!

Based on the tips here regarding installment and revolving debt, Harriet revises her entries, as follows: Her car payments stop in six months, so her total debt drops to $500. She recalculates her credit card debt at $150, or 5 percent of the balance, even though she usually pays at least $300.

Her total monthly debt of $350 is far less than the $750 she originally calculated. You'll soon see the dramatic impact of the reductions on her ability to buy her dream house.

INFLUENCE OF INCOME AND DEBT ON BORROWING POWER

The next stage of income/debt analysis is a quick calculation of borrowing power that is based simply on income in relation to three figures: the amount of down payment, estimated interest rate of the mortgage, and the term of the mortgage. This calculation highlights the *top ratio*, that is, the percentage of gross monthly income that the lender will allow for monthly housing costs.

To do a self-qualification highlighting your borrowing power on the basis of income and cash only, go to the Estimate module of the software. Any changes you make in the Income and Debt modules are automatically transferred if you save the changes.

Experiment. It is unlikely that a lender will do anything like this to help you.

Begin by entering the following:

- $100,000 for the purchase price. You will soon be adjusting this figure upward or downward.

- 20 percent *down payment*. Normally, 20 percent down is the minimum needed to avoid *mortgage insurance* or *private mortgage insurance*. Mortgage insurance protects the lender against default. You can estimate it at .53% of the loan amount per year, or $530 for a $100,000 loan (or $100,000 × .0053) with a monthly payment of roughly $40 that is rolled into the mortgage payment. The amount of the down payment gives you the *loan-to-value ratio*, or LTV. It means that, with a 20 percent down payment, the loan amount is 80 percent of the value of the property.

- 8 percent interest. It's a reasonable number to use for starters, based on the fluctuation in rates in the 1990s.

- $1,000 earnest money deposit. *Earnest money* is the deposit you give upfront when you tentatively commit to buying a property. It shows you mean business. This amount is added together with your down payment, and total due at closing, to arrive at a *total purchase cost*.

- $1,250 yearly real estate taxes. The tax rate used here is 1.25 percent. It can vary with location, but 1.25 is a good percentage for estimating. Similarly, use $1,250 for every $100,000.

- $30 monthly homeowner's insurance. This is estimated at .03 percent of the property value. [Note: If you want to accurately estimate insurance, multiply the purchase price by .0003. Otherwise, just use $30 for every $100,000.]

Now you are ready to play "if . . . then."

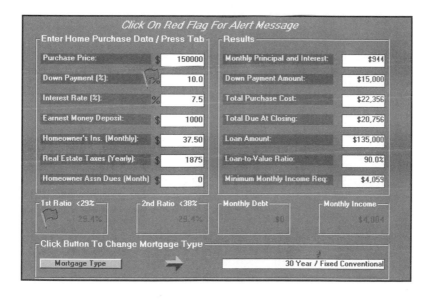

Enter Home Purchase Data / Press Tab		Results	
Purchase Price:	$ 100000	Monthly Principal and Interest:	$587
Down Payment (%):	% 20.0	Down Payment Amount:	$20,000
Interest Rate (%):	% 8.0	Total Purchase Cost:	$24,759
Earnest Money Deposit:	$ 1000	Total Due At Closing:	$23,159
Homeowner's Ins. (Monthly):	$ 22.5	Loan Amount:	$80,000
Real Estate Taxes (Yearly):	$ 1250	Loan-to-Value Ratio:	80.0%
Homeowner Assn Dues (Month):	$ 30	Minimum Monthly Income Req:	$2,656

1st Ratio <28%	2nd Ratio <36%	Monthly Debt	Monthly Income
7.44%	14.94%	$750	$10,000

Click Button To Change Mortgage Type

| Mortgage Type | ➡ | 30 Year / Fixed Conventional |

For a $100,000 purchase price, the screen now says you need a $20,000 down payment and thousands more for the total purchase cost. Keep adjusting the purchase price until the amount of money you have matches the amount in "total purchase cost."

Here is Harriet's result:

Click On Red Flag For Alert Message

Enter Home Purchase Data / Press Tab		Results	
Purchase Price:	$ 150000	Monthly Principal and Interest:	$944
Down Payment (%):	% 10.0	Down Payment Amount:	$15,000
Interest Rate (%):	% 7.5	Total Purchase Cost:	$22,356
Earnest Money Deposit:	$ 1000	Total Due At Closing:	$20,756
Homeowner's Ins. (Monthly):	$ 37.50	Loan Amount:	$135,000
Real Estate Taxes (Yearly):	$ 1875	Loan-to-Value Ratio:	90.0%
Homeowner Assn Dues (Month):	$ 0	Minimum Monthly Income Req:	$4,059

1st Ratio <29%	2nd Ratio <38%	Monthly Debt	Monthly Income
29.4%	29.4%	$0	$4,004

Click Button To Change Mortgage Type

| Mortgage Type | ➡ | 30 Year / Fixed Conventional |

Since Harriet's heart was set on a $150,000 house, she wondered what would happened if she put only 10 percent down. She also heard banks recently advertising 7.5 percent rates for home loans and thought, "Maybe I could get that." Those changes yielded the following results:

To view the breakdown of your monthly payment, that includes principal, interest, taxes, and insurance (PITI), including mortgage insurance if you must pay it, go to the Main Menu screen of the software. Use the first pull-down menu item, Estimate. This selects the option View Financing Estimate which allows you to review the breakdown.

Notice that Harriet's monthly principal and interest is not her entire payment. Because she must pay taxes and mortgage insurance, additional amounts of $156.25 ($1,875 divided by 12 months) and $39.38 must be added. The $39.38 is calculated as follows: Loan amount multiplied by .53 percent, or .00053. The result is then divided by 12 months.

Flags on the Estimate screen call attention to potential trouble spots. Click on a flag to bring up an explanation of the issue.

The flags on the estimate screen not only draw attention to the fact that Harriet must pay mortgage insurance, but also that her top ratio is a hair over the limit. Here is an example in which evidence of yearly salary increases would make a difference. By next year, Harriet will easily make the ratio.

The maximum purchase price of Harriet's house, based on these standard calculations is $150,000. Looks like she got her house! But not so fast. Harriet's debt could cause a detour.

Based on the guidelines used by lenders, her total allowable monthly debt would be limited to about $325. That simply means that her monthly estimated housing cost of $1,200 added to $325 should not exceed 38 percent of her income. That percent varies by lender and type of loan, but this is customary. This number is the *bottom ratio* or the percentage of gross monthly income that the lender will allow for monthly housing costs plus monthly debt.

When Harriet's debt sinks to $350 a month, or slightly lower if she documents a lower monthly payment on her credit cards than 5 percent of the balance, Harriet is prequalified for a $135,000 loan.

ASSETS, AND HOW TO APPLY THEM

Looks like Harriet can qualify for her dream house? Not exactly.

Her cash reserves are too low to satisfy a lender. After making the down payment and paying all the closing costs, including things like appraisal and inspection fees, Harriet will only have about $1,000 left. She'll need the equivalent of 3 month's PITI, or $3,400.

Her savings account contains $23,000, which is what she has listed as her available cash. A number of other sources of cash could be combined with that so she could end up with more cash reserves—maybe even a higher down payment:

- funds in checking, as well as savings, accounts
- stocks/bonds that can be liquidated
- cash gift from a relative
- net proceeds from the sale of real property
- proceeds from the sale of other assets
- other cash available

Harriet thinks about selling her skydiving equipment, but changes her mind. If she really needs more cash, she could sell some jewelry or ask her brother for a couple thousand dollars. In the meantime, how else could she use the money she has?

Harriet might want to put more money up front in *points*, a one-time charge by the lender to increase the yield of the loan, and less in down payment to try to reduce her interest rate. One point, which is 1 percent of the amount of the mortgage, would cost her $1,350 and is part of the closing costs. The lower interest rate would bring down her monthly payments.

She could also increase her *disposable income* by changing the amount of tax deducted from her paycheck. Since Harriet's monthly payments will largely be tax-deductible interest payments (in the early days of a mortgage, very little of the payment amount goes to principal), she will enjoy thousands in tax benefits. Her first year of payments alone should represent about a $2,500 tax break. The calculation of tax benefits is based on current tax laws, the individual's tax bracket, and other facts. You can use good tax preparation software and/or the services of a professional to get an accurate reading of the tax advantages of your mortgage.

COMMON-SENSE CRITERIA THAT AFFECT BORROWING POWER

As mentioned in Chapter 1, in the old-school of lending, bankers would rely on the *four Cs* to determine whether or not to grant a loan: credit, collateral, capacity, and character.

"Character" meant something like, "Sure, I'll give you a loan, Jack. I've known your father for 40 years, and if you are anything like him, you're a safe bet." Now, character relates to those few subjective aspects of the loan application that theoretically demonstrate stability, such as years of school.

Other factors involving a measure of character because they all relate to consistent behavior can actually give you an edge if you are close to making the *qualifying ratios*. These include a consistent pattern of accumulating assets, conservative use of consumer credit, steady history of employment, especially in the same field, and steady history of advancement in the same profession.

In a private, self-paced, self-qualifying process, you are free to ask questions and generate answers with an almost unlimited number of variables. You can become facile with the formulas and comfortable with the notion of manipulating the numbers to learn important facts about your financial leverage.

The powerful desire to purchase a home can create the result you want only if you act on it systematically and with an eye for opportunities. Focus on the vista! It will keep you justifiably hopeful as we go through the next segment of the Maze—credit reporting.

Chapter 3

A Smooth Road:
Keep the Records Clean

Keeping the records clean refers to the four, or more, different types of credit instruments, standard and non-traditional, that a lender can use to establish your borrowing status. You need the tools and techniques for taking charge of these credit records.

You can get your bureau credit reports quickly, grasp the relative significance of items on them, and effect change. Learn what the non-traditional, or alternate records are. The information on the non-traditional or alternate records can discolor the attractive picture your other reports create.

Lenders use "artificial intelligence" to analyze and assign a numerical score to your credit history and make you guilty until proven innocent when it comes to credit disputes. True stories will illustrate how disturbing errors find their way onto a credit report and what actions can remove them. Some solutions are common sense. Others are the result of experience. Both are labor intensive, either for you or the expert who helps you.

ARE CREDIT REPORTING AGENCIES REALLY THAT BAD?

Many people think of credit reporting agencies as servants of the devil. Their tools of torture are credit reports, foul documents, full of lies as well as the most painful truths. An exorcism is not required to do business with TRW Information Services Division, Trans Union Corporation, CBI/Equifax Credit Information Services, and their affiliates, such as Computer Sciences Corporation (CSC) Credit Services, a company in the Equifax network. In a sense, they are victims of annoying business practices, too. When the creditors, their clients who contribute to their databases, give them garbage information, they turn around and give the same garbage back to the consumer. It's very automatic. A process that is uninterrupted by human touch, kindness, malevolence, or insight.

TRUE STORY: MISLEADING LATE PAYMENTS CORRECTED

Rob Reynolds was stopped cold by a lender when his credit report turned up some 30-day-late payments on his current mortgage. Rob could not understand it: He had been 15 or 20 days late, but never 30. How could this happen?

Rob's mortgage holder routinely reported any payment made after the 15th of the month as a "late" to the credit bureau. Credit reporting bureaus don't have categories for 15 days late, or 23 days late, so Rob's delinquencies became "30 days late" by default.

In order to counter the information in the credit report, Rob had to retrieve years of canceled checks. Once the bureaus saw them, however, they were obligated by law to erase the misleading designations.

Credit reporting agencies record, organize and analyze information in a rigid fashion, then provide the end result to companies that subscribe to their service. They are not in business to scar consumers emotionally or financially. They manage data—period. To the computers at a credit reporting agency, you are nothing more than a faceless being who resides somewhere in the United States and spends money through the use of credit in a particular pattern.

It is when you have a problem with what the computer outputs that you suddenly come alive for the reporting agency. Human beings work in their customer service departments, and to them, you are an individual whose right to know and to dispute your record is articulated by federal law. These people are there to help you. Treat them with respect and they will treat you likewise. They have the ability to guide you through the credit report section of the Mortgage Maze.

Credit is not a legal right; it is earned. Once you have earned it, however, you do have the legal right to protect your credit and demand that all records relating to it are accurate.

You can stop the cycle of "garbage in, garbage out" that affects your credit report. You can make certain your credit report is a fair representation of your record. From a psychological point of view, you can move past unreasonable, as well as reasonable, fears about dealing with reporting agencies and other repositories of credit information.

A Close Look at Credit Bureau Reports

To many potential mortgage holders, the most stressful and confusing leg of the road toward home ownership is the credit reporting exercise. It is the Maze Master's experience that 8 out of 10 potential borrowers wince when they hear, "I'll have to get a copy of your credit report." One out of 10 doesn't know enough to care, and the other one is too rich to care.

True Story: Post-Dated Check Saved by the System

When Roger and Carol Aaron held their flawless credit report in their hands, they were visibly relieved. It was as if the mortgage broker had just delivered a perfect baby into their arms. They had feared the report would reveal a problem.

A month before, Carol had sent a post-dated check to cover her bank card payment. She knew if the check were cashed upon receipt, the funds would not yet be available. She thought post-dating would avert a problem. Since logging and depositing payments is another automatic function in the credit process, no one held Carol's check. When Carol called customer service to explain what she had done and how much trouble a dishonored check caused her, the representative gave her a demeaning lecture on the illegality of writing a post-dated check. Carol was terrified. She was sure the nitpicker in customer service would insert a derogatory remark on her credit report.

Carol and Roger were safe because the process is so automatic. Although their check was dishonored when first presented, the creditor automatically presented it a second time, when sufficient funds were in the Aaron's account. It all happened within the "grace period" automatically allowed by virtually all creditors, so there was no record of a late payment. The customer service representative could not have broken the cycle even if she'd wanted to do it.

Explaining the blotches on a credit record can be the ultimate test of your commitment to owning a home, because there are so many things that can go wrong. In some cases, it's more complicated than the Rob Reynolds story where a pattern of misleading reporting by a lender could be defined and corrected.

The field of credit reporting is replete with bizarre mistakes, errors that involve no pattern, because there are so many types of information going into credit records. A name change after marriage or divorce, two identical names or addresses, a mis-typed middle initial, or a slip in recording a social security number are just some of the situations that can lead to erroneous entries on a report, or to the accidental creation of an entirely new credit file. If you're thinking "What a great way to start over," it is not. And regardless of the fact that bureaus are obligated by law to treat both the credit grantor and consumer fairly, the consumer is still guilty until proven innocent when it comes to disputes. The credit grantor, after all, is the bureau's client.

TRUE STORY: SAME NAME, WRONG DATA

Jane P. Bradley, a receptionist, was delighted that her application for a department store card had been approved with the high credit ceiling. It was her first card, and she used it often—too often. Her income allowed her to pay only the monthly minimum, and she had run up quite a balance. Jane P. Bradley, a lawyer, sought a copy of her credit report when she planned to buy a new house. She noticed that the store where she once had an account, but had closed it, was reporting her as owing a balance of $1,476. Yes, it belonged to the other Jane P. Bradley in a distant city.

And what about the receptionist's credit report? It showed no record of her transactions, unfortunately. Even a minimum monthly payment, if it's paid as agreed, is a plus on a report.

The lender, too, is the bureau's client, either directly or through a service that consolidates credit information from multiple sources. These services can provide the lender with an RMCR and credit score. A standardized report, called a Residential Mortgage Credit Report or RMCR, shows how religiously the potential borrower has repaid debts, particularly in the past 24 months. Credit grantors and credit scoring companies look closest at the most current rolling 24 months for prediction of future risk. Most importantly, the lender wants to see whether the prospective borrower has ever been late with a mortgage payment; that is the ultimate case of bad maneuvering in the Mortgage Maze. A credit score rates the potential borrower's activity to help the lender determine objectively whether a person is a good credit prospect or a bad one.

If the sole service requested by a lender is the RMCR, then an individual's judgment of your creditworthiness can influence the ultimate lending decision. *Credit scoring* is an alternative to that conventional method that makes analysis of your report, on a bureau-by-bureau basis, a purely objective process. This can be good and bad, from a potential borrower's point of view.

For example, using the conventional method, a loan officer may feel the number of *inquiries* about your credit that have been made in the past six months is insignificant because of the sources. Perhaps the sources were prospective employers and department stores, which typically have a lower ceiling and more limited use than a bank card. On the other hand, credit scoring would automatically assign points according to the number of inquiries. Zero inquiries might merit 50 points, whereas five or more would merit none. If the ideal score is 900 points, therefore, a flawless record of payment would be tarnished because you sought additional credit from a handful of companies.

Conversely, if a health care facility won a judgment against you four years ago, a lender would require an explanation, and might give undue weight to the problem regardless of the explanation. Your credit score would reflect less impact, however, because of the age of the derogatory record. Out of a possible 75 points, you may score 55. There are more details about scoring and its importance at the end of the chapter.

The standardized nature of both credit reporting and credit scoring gives the lender a measure of security in the loan process, security that the same criteria of creditworthiness are used for each and every potential borrower. Oddly enough, while it is obvious how this standardization can prevent certain prejudicial decisions on the part of lenders, consumers often view it as a source of anxiety. It is a prime example of the nameless, faceless, impersonal set of challenges you face in the Mortgage Maze.

Once you break the code, you can break the cycle of stress. You can get your credit report, read it, get a feel for your score and how to improve it, and dispute and correct errors. The alternative is to enter the Mortgage Maze unaware, drive down that bumpy, winding credit trail, then get stuck trying to fix your car in the dark.

REQUESTING YOUR CREDIT REPORT

Because credit reporting is a standardized activity, it is a perfect candidate for computer-based solutions, like setting up a template for letters to bureaus or using Internet resources to contact bureaus or request a credit report.

 You can also use the Internet Web site www.maze.com to request your credit report. This will cost you about $30 and will include a consolidated report similar to the lender's RMCR and your credit score. The credit score will not be supplied to you when requesting a single report from a credit bureau. Just click on the "Mortgage Services" button on the main menu, then click on "Credit Report" and follow instructions.

When you go directly to an individual credit bureau with a request, the credit report you request is not identical to the RMCR, which lenders incorporate into your loan package. Neither is the credit score included. As mentioned above, an RMCR is prepared by a service that consolidates credit information from multiple repositories. Whichever path you choose, you will need to supply the following information:

- Complete name

- Date of birth

- Social Security number

- Current address

- Previous address(es) to create a record of where you have lived for the past five years

- Your spouse's first name, if married. TRW lists this as "necessary information."

If you are willing to contact the three bureaus yourself, follow three sets of rules, and wait about three weeks for a response, the cost is as follows:

- TRW provides one free credit report per year. Others may soon adopt this policy.

- Anyone denied credit in the last 60 days can also get a free copy. Send a copy of your declination letter with your request.

- If these two options do not apply, there is a small fee to get the report. The usual cost is $8 per report if you go directly to each and every bureau. This may change depending on your state of residence, as follows:

- For Maryland and Vermont residents, the first copy of your credit report is free. Every copy after that in Maryland is no more than $5.25; in Vermont, it's $7.50.

- Maine residents pay no more than $3 a copy.

- The fee is higher if you go through a credit repair business or a Web service that consolidates reports, and counsels you on problems and correcting errors. Beware if the fee is hundreds of dollars, however! There are credit-repair scams that carry high price tags.

The individual bureau's requirements and allowances could change at any time, so call the bureau and listen to the recorded instructions, or go to their home pages on the World Wide Web.

The phone numbers for the main credit reporting companies are as follows:

CBI/Equifax	TRW	Trans Union
800-685-1111	800-682-7654	800-296-0112 (IL)
		800-8512674 (CA)

Whether you file your request by mail, fax or automated phone service, it will probably take two weeks to a month to receive your report. Contacting Equifax-affiliate CSC directly at 800-759-5979 will expedite service if you live in an area covered by CSC, which is headquartered in Texas and has operations in 15 states.

If you want to order a consolidated credit report and your credit score from www.maze.com via the telephone (not a computer), call 888-552-5626 (LOAN).

UNDERSTANDING YOUR CREDIT REPORT

Your credit report from an agency like Trans Union, TRW, Equifax or their affiliates has four main sections. The actual report formats vary a little from company to company, but they contain the same summary information, as follows:

Identifying Information. Name; current and previous addresses; social security number; date of birth; employment information.

Trade Lines, which are Paid As Agreed, Zero Balance or Closed Accounts, and Derogatory Trade Items. Date reported; date opened; highest credit approved (Some companies report only highest credit used, even though your limit may be higher.); current balance; type—revolving [R], installment [I], or cleared monthly [CLR]; current rating, with R1 or I1 the best and R9 or I9 the worst; current payment status; historical delinquency information (The *date of last delinquency*, or DLD, indicates if you were ever late with a payment.).

Inquiries. Requests for credit data by a credit grantor in response to a consumer's application; requests for credit data by a prospective employer.

Public Record and Collection Items. *Judgments*; *liens*; *collection items*; *bankruptcy*.

Credit reports list the types of credit in use: installment loans, revolving accounts and *cleared monthly accounts* or CLRs, such as American Express Company and many gas company accounts that must be paid in full upon receipt of each statement. They also list the length of time these accounts have been open, date the account was reported last or last activity, and your payment patterns during the most recent period of activity. They indicate how much of the credit available to you has been used and if you have recently authorized any potential creditor, like a bank or clothing store, to review your record.

If you are even daydreaming about homeownership in the near future, watch how you handle credit cards and requests for credit. Do not use your credit cards to the limit. Credit reports don't reflect your payments or your restraint at the moment: They show what you did 30 to 60 days ago. You cannot think, "I'll make the report look good by bringing the balance down when I apply for the loan." It will be a month or two before your creditor reports current activity to the credit bureau. As a corollary, if you delay buying that new wardrobe until after you apply for the loan, don't assume your extravagance is your secret. Here's why. A lender may do an employment check and order an *HUP*, the industry slang for "hurry up credit report," the day your loan is supposed to be funded. This is a standard quality-control measure of most lenders, and it is the moment when your spending sprees could be noticed. Finally, if there are new inquiries from credit grantors on your report, the lender might follow up to see if you have established any new accounts. New balances will be added to your debt ratios, which could reverse the lender's decision minutes before closing!

TRUE STORY: THE LAST MINUTE REJECTION

Lynn Brady's mortgage process dragged on for nearly four months because of structural flaws with the property. Finally they were corrected, and the transaction could move forward. On the closing day everything was coming together quickly. Only two details remained: Money had to be wired from New York so the close could take place, and the lender had to complete the last-minute checks on credit and employment.

In doing the final quality-control review, the lender found out Ford Credit had made an inquiry about Lynn's credit. A call to Ford confirmed that Lynn had, indeed, bought a car two weeks ago. Her ratios changed enough to give the lender heartburn, but he was inclined to proceed. He made the final call to verify employment. The human resources director told the lender something that Lynn was finding out at that moment: this was her last day on the job. Without further ado, the deal was off. You're not safe from a lender's scrutiny until the ink is dry on the paperwork.

THE LENDER'S RED FLAGS

If you can't get past "Identifying Information" in your understanding of the report, you are in the majority. Jumbled formats and arcane codes make most credit reports confusing. As you go through your report, check for the codes and words that raise red flags for lenders. Red flags include charge offs, coll acct, 00/00/00, judgments, liens, and R1-R9. These items are all referred to on the Sample Credit Report from www.maze.com.

Charge off. A charge off means your creditor gave up on you and closed the account without receiving the balance due. When the creditor takes this action, the automatic rating is an R9. R1 is the best. In addition, you will have a charge-off amount and penalties in the past-due column of your credit report. A mortgage lender rarely allows a past-due amount to stand while the loan goes through; you'll have to pay it.

Coll acct. Short for *collection account*, this term means your creditor gave up on you and made you a collection agent's problem. Collection agencies generally earn 50 percent of the amount they collect. The remedy is so costly for the credit grantor that, again, the action automatically assigns an R9 rating to the account. And, again, just because the credit grantor stopped trying to collect the money does not mean you don't owe it anymore.

Delinquency. Numbers, other than zero, in the sequence 00/00/00 (often separated by slashes) refer to the number of times you had a delinquency of 30, 60, or 90 days. The sequence 01/01/00 means you had one 30-day, one 60-day and no 90-day delinquencies with a particular account. It is common for a 01/01/00 sequence, for example, to refer to the same delinquency, rather than one 30-day and a separate 60-day late. Called a *rolling late*, the problem can arise and persist when you are 30 days late with a January payment, for instance, then make a payment in February that is automatically credited to February. When you make a payment in March, your January payment is still considered delinquent and it would "roll over" into the 60-day category.

Lien, Judgment. Phrases in the public document section such as "lien filed" or "judgment decreed" that are not followed by the word "released" or "satisfied" are red flags to lenders. The same lien can appear multiple times. A lien expires after a period of time, and when the credit grantor files it again with a new amount reflecting additional interest and fees, the lien is assigned a new case number and more lines on your credit report.

Codes R1-R9. Bureaus use codes R1 to designate your achievement of perfection with a particular revolving account, such as a bank card, and I1, which indicates the same for an installment account, such as an auto loan. An R9 means your creditor has condemned you to credit purgatory.

When an R9 or I9 is paid in full, it still appears on your credit report for up to 7 years unless the credit grantor instructs the credit bureau to remove it. You need to get the creditor's commitment in writing to give you leverage with the credit bureau in case there is a delay or problem. You must negotiate in advance with the creditor if you expect to get it removed from the credit report.

A single R5 often indicates a unique situation. R5 designates a 150- to 180-day delinquency, which may arise because the consumer has taken a righteous stand against the system. If you bought a couch that was defective, for example, and returned it to the store with a request for a replacement, you might contest, "I don't have to make the payments on something I don't have." Unfortunately, you do unless the vendor who extended you the credit notifies you in writing that payments have been suspended pending resolution of your claim. If you wait six months for your order, then begin making payments, your account may have earned R5 status before you ever sit down on your new couch.

TRUE STORY: FIRE DAMAGES CREDIT TEMPORARILY

Jerry Birch's new house burned to the ground in a fire that consumed thousands of acres near Oakland, California. Although he and his neighbors had hazard insurance, his situation with his mortgage company differed from theirs. It threw him into financial chaos without him knowing it.

After the tragedy, most lenders serving the affected residents declared a payment moratorium on mortgages. It was both a practical move, reflecting the time delays inherent in most insurance transactions, and a public relations ploy. Television reporters happily announced that the stricken homeowners had been given a break by the banks.

Jerry's mortgage company, unlike the others, expected payments as usual. It had to be shamed into joining those lenders that had declared a payment moratorium. It took months, and in the meantime, even though there was nothing left of his house but a charred spot, Jerry was required to pay the mortgage as agreed if he wanted to preserve his good credit. By the time he realized that fact, the damage to his record had been done. After Jerry protested, one of the loan officers at the bank assured him the lates would disappear from his credit report. Weeks later, Jerry got the promise in writing and started the long process or repairing his record.

TRUE STORY: CREDIT REPORT OFFERS
MORE THAN FINANCIAL FACTS

Susan Lewis Bentley and Rick Bentley, newlyweds of five weeks, visited their local mortgage broker with the intention of buying a new home. When their broker requested the HUPs, or hurry up credit reports, on both parties, she had a surprise and so did Rick. Susan's report indicated several derogatory items along with a "J," a "CS" and an "AU," meaning that someone else had held a joint account with her, was a co-signer on a loan, and was an authorized user of one of her accounts, respectively. In addition, there was an aka ("also known as") that was not Susan Lewis.

The broker left the room as Susan began explaining to Rick that she had been married before.

Once you have ascertained where the blemishes are, your focus should be on the report dates. Keep in mind several different time frames.

- 6 months. Inquiries for your credit information from prospective credit grantors can, but don't necessarily, stay on your report for this length of time.

- 24 months. Inquiries for your credit information from prospective employers can, but don't necessarily, stay on your report for this long.

- 24 months. This is the period scrutinized by lenders.

- 7 years. Trade information, including accounts charged off or placed in collection, should be off the report when they are 7 years old.

- 7 years. Paid tax liens should be off the report after this period of time.

- 7 years. Information on lawsuits or judgments against you can be reported for 7 years or until the statute of limitations expires, whichever is longer.

- 10 years. This is the length of time a bankruptcy can stay on the report.

Here are two final notes about possible unpleasant surprises on the credit report.

1. Like the rude driver who cuts you off when you're trying to change lanes, some companies report delinquency information on your worst behavior in the history of your account. In other words, if you were 90 days late with one payment six years ago, there is probably a reference to it in your bureau report.

2. The 7- and 10-year periods noted above refer to that last date of activity in some cases. If you paid a collection agent the amount

in full a couple years after the R9 first appeared on your record, for example, the clock may have started again from the date of the last payment or the date it was paid in full.

Your recourse in both cases is to ask the creditor to have the derogatory note removed.

PROBLEMS AND THEIR IMPACT ON YOUR BORROWING POWER

While the "good old days" of borrowing are gone, there are still some similarities between past and present. Bankruptcy, slow pay, exceeding your credit limit, collection accounts, charge offs, and public records can be problems which will impact on your borrowing power.

Bankruptcy. To start, take bankruptcy. It used to doom you with a lender, and it still could unless it's managed well. There has been an exponential rise in the number of individuals, as well as corporations, using bankruptcy laws as part of their financial strategy rather than out of sheer desperation. In 1995, individual bankruptcies in the United States ran at the rate of nearly two filings per minute! That year more than 800,000 people sought bankruptcy versus 80,000 in 1958, according to federal statistics.

While a bankruptcy does stay on your credit report for 10 years, it does not necessarily dissolve your credit and capacity. A CLR account or "cleared monthly account", such as American Express, might be handled outside a Chapter 11 bankruptcy, giving you the ability to demonstrate on-time paying during your period of financial reorganization. On the other hand, a Chapter 7 bankruptcy signals total inability to handle payments.

Regardless of the type, you do have a right to annotate your file with a brief explanation, such as "Bankruptcy followed embezzlement by business partner" or "Bankruptcy brought on by death of spouse after lingering illness depleted all accounts." As long as your explanation is verifiable, and you have evidence that you are steadily rebuilding your financial health, a lender might opt to grant the loan despite your setback.

Here is a case-by-case look at other credit problems and their importance.

TRUE STORY: A BANKRUPTCY IS A BANKRUPTCY

Max Karli owed $122,000 when he declared bankruptcy. Rather than negotiate with any of his creditors, however, he paid 100 percent of what he owed over a 6-year period. This is rare: Individuals and companies that declare bankruptcy generally pay creditors only a portion of what is owed; many creditors assume that the bankrupt individual is good for only 40 or 50 cents on the dollar.

Max went to a lender to get a mortgage at the end of his grueling six years of payments. The bankruptcy was still on his record. It made absolutely no difference to the lender that Max paid everyone every dime he owed. To the lender, a bankruptcy is a bankruptcy.

As honest as he was, Max's record did not distinguish him because he took no steps to impress upon the lender that his record was any different from anyone else who had declared bankruptcy.

Slow pay. There is a big difference between a consistent slow payer and an occasional slow payer. Someone with plenty of money who routinely doesn't pay bills on time is a bad risk. On the other hand, occasional slow payers often have legitimate excuses for their delays. It is easy to soothe a lender concerned about lates if they never applied to a mortgage, and if one of the following circumstances exists: (1) all happened in a concentrated period such as during an illness, (2) they related to only one account and you were unaware of a rolling late, or (3) they were sporadic and you thought you made late-payment arrangements, but lates were nevertheless reported by the creditor.

TRUE STORY: GET IT IN WRITING

Craig Perkins anticipated hard times when his company, a major computer manufacturer, laid him off. His severance package enabled him to make timely mortgage payments for six months and pay minimums due on major credit cards, but he knew he would fall behind on the payments for his Jaguar. In the interest of preserving his good credit, he called the financing company and spoke with a very accommodating woman. "Would it be okay if I delayed payments for two months, while I search for a comparable position?" he asked. She replied, "Sure. I'll log your request. There shouldn't be a problem. It's people who don't call who have a problem."

Well, that's not necessarily so. As Craig found out, if the financing company's computer does not have a record of an actual payment, it automatically reports to the credit bureau's computer that Craig Perkins is 30 days late. Then 60 days late. This is one version of what the industry calls artificial intelligence. The computer doesn't care if Craig took the time to notify customer service that a payment would be delayed.

Craig's only recourse was to document that he spoke with a representative named Alice Parker at 10 AM on March 12, 1996, and that she advised him he would not be penalized for the 60-day delay he requested. If Craig did not have that information, his claim would have been suspect.

A quick way to document the call is to ask the representative to fax a note on company letterhead that reiterates the terms of the agreement.

Exceedingly Slow Pay. As indicated above, the R5 rating for late payment of at least 150 days is often the result of a misunderstanding between a vendor and a consumer. Any other reason for it better be tied to nuclear war or an invasion from Mars, because lenders find it hard to believe a good credit risk could be several months late paying bills.

Exceeding Your Credit Limit. Many of you will remember the old days of credit cards, when authorization was made by the clerk at the counter, or at the pump by the service station attendant, or by the waitress at the table. Then, you could "fudge" your limit. Now, everyone is familiar with the electronic devices that instantly log your expenditures. Running from one bar to another and charging Dom Perignon no longer works unless your bankcard company's computer says you can afford the Dom Perignon every step of the way. How then, can you exceed your credit limit, an act that seriously disturbs a lender?

That little boat you want costs $11,000, and you have a new VISA card with a $10,000 limit and low introductory rate of 5.9% interest for the first year. You make a $1,200 down payment on the boat and calculate that the balance will incur less interest if you charge it, and pay the bill in 12 months, than if you use other financing options. Unfortunately, even at a low rate, the interest on the balance due kicks you over your credit limit—a fact duly noted on your credit report.

The minimum monthly payment due on a credit card account may be less than an interest-only payment. Therefore, you can repeatedly make the minimum payment, and even with no new purchases, see an increase in your balance.

Collection. As with an R5, if your account has gone to a collection agency, you may well have taken a righteous stand against a vendor because of defective merchandise or unacceptable service. Nevertheless, it's a serious problem until strong documentation counters its merit. The lender looks at this as a financial obligation that you signed up for and that you are not honoring "as agreed." You may find yourself forced into a corner by a lender who considers paying the old debt a condition of getting your loan. Lenders don't like to see members of the brotherhood burned.

Charge Offs. Lenders assume that charge offs indicate total lack of responsibility on the part of the borrower. Sometimes, however, they arise from accounting mistakes and the bad record is just another example of how artificial intelligence—one computer zapping data to another without human intervention—makes a mess of your credit.

Public records. This is an area where artificial intelligence can break down. In contrast to the electronic data transmission that occurs with credit card accounts, the damning information in public records can come from courthouses where paper still rules. For that reason, inaccuracies in the amounts, dates, and so on, are not uncommon. There have even been cases in which bankruptcies showed up that had no relationship to the credit holder. If there is a public record in your report, examine it very carefully.

Reliability aside, public records are alarming to lenders because they define the individual as a bad planner or irresponsible slouch, at best. They could also mean the person is a con artist or a pathological liar.

In some cases, the public record is just a cruel reminder of a tax debt that you are scrupulously addressing. Even if you have a payment agreement with the IRS, you may have a tax lien on your credit report.

Keep these three things in mind regarding liens: (1) If the problem expressed in your record is legitimate, your best recourse is to have evidence that you handled it legally and consistently. Save your canceled checks and all correspondence. (2) The maximum amount of time a paid lien can remain on your credit report is seven years. (3) If a lien remains unpaid at the time your mortgage documents come under scrutiny by the lender, you may be required to eliminate it prior to closing.

In short, when evaluating your RMCR through a lender's eyes, look at these problems from top to bottom:

Payment History

- Public Records and Collection Items

- Delinquencies

- How late were your lates?

- Were they recent, in the past 24 months?

- Were you a consistent late-payer, or an occasional one?

Outstanding Debt

- Number of balances reported

- Average balances

- Relationship between average balances and credit limits

Inquiries and New Accounts

- Number of inquiries in the last 2–3 months

- Number of new accounts in the last year

How Much Credit Should You Have?

How many accounts of each type do you have? Two or three in well-maintained accounts in each category—bank card, travel card, department store account, installment loans—is rather standard, but a handful of each would raise questions.

True Story: Relax, There's Always Another Bank

Gary Hernandez had a pristine credit record. Even after he was stricken with cancer and couldn't work, he paid bills on time out of his savings. Eventually, to keep his business alive, he had to use all available sources of credit. He had three employees who depended on him for their livelihood. He exploited his perfect credit record by accepting offers of new lines of credit and bank cards that routinely came in the mail, and amassed $125,000 in revolving credit. Gary continued to make minimum payments to the creditors and kept his record clean. Unfortunately, by the time surgery and radiation treatments proved successful and he returned to work full-time, Gary had the daunting task of paying off $38,000 in credit card bills. Interest on the accounts ranged from 8 to 18 percent.

He went to a local bank to borrow the money at a lower interest rate. A $40,000 loan would have allowed him to consolidate his debt, and stop the ravaging by his credit card companies. After commending Gary on his obvious triumph over financial and medical adversity, the loan officer turned him down for the loan. Gary had made all payments on time, all the time, but his overuse of credit made him sink to ranks of the unworthy in the banker's eyes.

Gary is a mortgage broker who tells this story to his clients as a way of saying, "Relax. Sometimes you get bad treatment even if you do everything in your power to handle things responsibly. There's always another bank."

The key message regarding credit problems is this: The severe objectivity of the current mortgage process has not given rise to new categories of credit problems. It has merely made the documentation and explanation of problems more central to the process. People with a rocky credit history can get mortgages, and people with bogus entries on their reports can get them removed.

In fact, it is often people with no credit who have a larger obstacle to bypass in the Mortgage Maze. Nearly all of the people with no credit had serious problems more than seven years ago, and they never took the steps to reestablish themselves. True, there are those people in all parts of the country who have always lived life on a cash basis, but they aren't concerned with getting a mortgage. They probably inherited a nice two-bedroom place from their parents. To get a mortgage, you must be able to show that you have a credit record. Go to Chapter 4 if you need to investigate nontraditional approaches.

Now look at alternate sources of your credit information, and you'll become more familiar with how the RMCR can be enhanced or destroyed in a moment.

WHAT ARE THOSE OTHER CREDIT RECORDS?

On the positive side, some credit records are in your grasp that you can add to your mortgage file to prove you are a consistent, capable payer. They include canceled checks for utility bills, rent, loans from small credit unions, or payments to other institutions that do not automatically report to credit bureaus. Utility companies and phone companies may not report your consistent, or inconsistent, payment to credit bureaus, but they do provide documentation of your creditworthiness by waiving deposits, for example, as well as noting your recent history in letters.

Records that are not in your grasp, those sought by the squint-eyed lender who thinks there must be a flaw in everyone's financial history, are: the *preliminary title report, verification of mortgage*, and *demand for pay-off*.

If you are a first-time home buyer, the preliminary title report, verification of mortgage, and demand for pay-off are not potential potholes for you. On the other hand, if you are moving from one mortgage to another, consider the unwelcome surprises they can contain.

How many people hire a carpenter or electrician to do work on a house, only to have a dispute about quality or timeliness arise?

Whether the problem stems from a misunderstanding, or unequiv-
ocal dissatisfaction with the product, the result is often the same.
The disgruntled contractor, who did not get the full payment, files a
mechanics lien. And where does that show up? In your preliminary
title report. The vendor who supplied the materials used in a reno-
vation that you find unsatisfactory may also file a mechanics lien.
His vinyl siding is on your house and, as bad as it looks, he wants to
be paid for it. In addition to mechanics liens, the preliminary title
report would also show delinquency in tax payments.

A verification of mortgage substitutes for, or in some cases aug-
ments, the payment information in a bureau credit report. First of
all, lenders don't necessarily report your mortgage-payment patterns
to a bureau. For example, Home Savings of America does not report.
In general, its customers must send a verification of mortgage to the
institution so that the new lender has evidence of the borrower's
payment history. The advantage for Home Savings is that receipt of
the verification alerts the company that one of its customers is looking elsewhere for a loan.

Even if your current mortgage company reports your payment
history, that is no guarantee the prospective lender will be satisfied
with a bureau report. A verification of mortgage may still be
required. If so, whereas the bureau report may indicate "no lates," the
verification of mortgage could provide greater detail indicating that
you have lates, but they are less than 30 days.

 If you want to avoid processing a verification of mortgage or verification of rent, submit 12 months of canceled checks.

If you are refinancing, a demand for pay-off is requested by the
title company to ascertain the exact amount you owe on your property. It would reflect your current lender's contention about any late
fees owed. So, if you always paid your mortgage within the month,
thereby avoiding "late" entries on your credit report, but did not pay
the late fees associated with a 15-day delay, your lender has a right to
demand payment before you enter into a new loan agreement.

Of course, sometimes the late fees are bogus. You may have made
perfectly legitimate arrangements with customer service to have late
fees waived, because of extended travel overseas or some other

extenuating circumstances. Unfortunately, the pay-off department doesn't necessarily talk to the customer service department.

THE STRAIGHT PATH TO CORRECTING ERRORS

Strengthened consumer-protection statutes, such as the Fair Credit Reporting Act, have made it cheaper and easier for you to get and correct your credit report than it used to be. Prior to the Act, effective April 1971, consumers had reasons to feel victimized by the credit reporting system.

 The law is also very clear about prohibitions against discrimination for any reason. The Equal Credit Opportunity Act says that, as long as you have the capacity to enter into a binding agreement, you must be considered fairly for credit. If you feel a lender has discriminated against you, seek legal aid.

Key advantages created by the Fair Credit Reporting Act include:

- Automatic elimination of aged accounts. After 6 years and 9 months, negative facts about your revolving, installment and cleared monthly accounts should begin to disappear. They had better be gone at the 7-year mark. After 10 years, the record of a bankruptcy must be removed. Lawsuits and judgments should be dropped after 7 years, or when the statute of limitations runs out.

- An immediate descriptive change from "derogatory" to "disputed" for credit items on your report that you have questioned.

- A timely response to your dispute. Generally, this means about 30 days, but the bureaus are caught in the creditors' timetables, too, so it could be longer. Don't tolerate delays. Sample dispute letter two in Appendix B is specifically designed as a follow-up to an unanswered dispute.

- A timely correction, if warranted. The law states that, in the case of disputed accuracy, the reporting agency "shall within a reasonable period of time re-investigate and record the current status of that information unless it has reasonable grounds to believe that the dispute by the consumer is frivolous or irrelevant. If after such reinvestigation such information is found to be inaccurate or can no longer be verified, the consumer reporting agency shall promptly delete such information." What are the problems with this provision? Define "reasonable." Define "promptly." Your persistence could create an acceptable definition.

The procedure to effect a correction in your credit report is very straightforward:

- Send the reporting agency a letter specifying what is incorrect about each record you dispute. Is the information outdated? Is the amount incorrect? Does the account belong to someone else? Templates of dispute letters and follow-up notices to the credit reporting agencies can be found in Appendix B and at web sites such as www.maze.com.

- The agency should log your dispute on your report and begin an investigation promptly. If you do not have evidence that any action has been taken within two weeks, send a follow-up letter requesting prompt cooperation.

- Keep the heat on until your report is accurate. This may mean more letters and more phone calls, but you will get satisfaction if your claim can be substantiated.

You have another important right under the law that can affect your status with a lender. If a credit agency is guilty of willful or negligent noncompliance with the law regarding the reporting of your credit, the agency is liable for damages you have sustained.

When you are waiting for a corrected and clean credit report in order to negotiate hard with a lender, you may find that nothing the bureau does is done fast enough. Save your canceled checks and correspondence so you have, at your fingertips, reliable documentation of your claim that you paid bills in dispute.

There are companies that have delivered on their promise to eradicate problems of all kinds on credit records. For a fee, sometimes thousands of dollars, these companies have established completely new credit files for their clients, who were plagued by bankruptcy, tax liens, and other devastating financial problems.

But you need to know that:

1. No one can require a credit reporting agency to remove accurate information that meets the time criterion.

2. The deliberate establishment of alternate credit files is fraud.

Using another name or social security number to establish a separate credit record is never legal, and the companies that use these tactics should always be avoided. Their scam could put you in jail.

If you think it is hard to establish a new credit file, either deliberately or inadvertently through a recording error, consider this fact. There are about six times the number of credit files as there are credit worthy people in the United States.

DRESSING UP BAD NEWS

After a bankruptcy, the lender takes a very close look at how the borrower has handled finances in the recent past. Depending on your actions over the past 12 to 24 months, you may have made great strides. Reestablishing old accounts, establishing a solid record with new accounts, regular contributions to a savings plan, payroll deductions that go into your children's college fund—all of these actions indicate a strategy for financially healing and compensate somewhat for the bankruptcy.

Similarly, if you had lots of slow pays or collection accounts just a few years ago, but your recent record is good, make those newer numbers seem even stronger. Use the documentation discussed in Chapter 4 to show that your utilities, phone, insurance and other non-reported accounts have also been paid on time in the recent past.

Another tactic that helps anyone plagued by credit problems who wants to demonstrate creditworthiness is to get a secured credit card, or debt card. A bankruptcy or a record of seriously slow pays and collections is like a dead skunk in the middle of the road to credit card companies. They want to get as far away from you as possible. A number of banks, however, will provide you with a "credit" card that operates like an automated teller machine or ATM card. Although the limit is tied to the amount of money available, just as a check is, the record of payment on the account is reported like that of any credit card. You can build good credit without having any credit extended to you. If you have had credit problems, no doubt one of the banks that offers this service has sent you a promotional mailing or will in the near future. This is not a scam. This is a legitimate method of rebuilding your credit.

TRUE STORY: REBUILDING CREDIT

After doing substandard work on a couple key contracts, Marie Villik's business partner siphoned off most of the remaining company assets before he walked out. This left her with loans and credit card debts to pay off. She was a very slow payer in this period and finally decided, unwisely, to stabilize her debt by closing all credit card accounts.

Three years later, when she finished paying off the accounts, her creditors were satisfied, but her record was such a mess that no one would reestablish her accounts. When she got a job that required travel, she was repeatedly embarrassed because she had no credit card to secure her hotel and car reservations. Marie got a secured credit card with a mere $250 investment. Her credit was limited to that amount, but at least she had made a start. She always made payments on time, and that fact was reported to the credit bureau. Less than a year later, offers began coming to her from companies willing to extend credit. She qualified for a $500 limit with one company. A year later, she had a card with a $10,000 limit.

CREDIT SCORING: WHY IS THE MAGIC FORMULA SUCH A SECRET?

You've seen the words "artificial intelligence" used in these pages before, and probably wondered if the Maze Master hadn't misappropriated them. Actually, it is a term-of-art in finance, as well as computer science, and it refers to the "smart" way computers manage and make sense of the many bits of disconnected data that affect a person's financial picture. This is most evident in the area of credit scoring.

As a consumer, you have heard of TRW, Trans Union, and Equifax, but it's unlikely you're familiar with Fair Isaac, Empirica, and Beacon. The latter are not credit reporting agencies, they are *credit information services* that assign a score to your credit record.

The systems of weighted variables that are integral to scoring are closely guarded. They are proprietary methodologies developed by analyzing millions of records to determine commonalities and differences in credit performances. Theoretically, each of the scoring methodologies that emerged from this process removes any bias from credit analysis. A good score is earned by the numbers, with absolutely no relationship to what company financed your car, where you live, what your last name sounds like, or which department stores you frequent. Subscribers to the service find this appealing, because it ensures compliance with the law at the same time it offers enormous potential for reducing risk. They are willing to pay well for this insurance, which is why the companies that developed these formulas keep them secret. In other words, it's not so much that the services don't want consumers to understand the basis for their scores as it is that they don't want new competitors gnawing away at their business. When you order a credit report from the credit bureaus, you will not find your credit scores reported. These scores are available as tools for mortgage determinations by the lenders. However, the merged credit report available to you from www.maze.com reports a Beacon credit score.

While retail companies and banks sometimes use scoring as the primary factor in deciding to extend credit, the mortgage lender uses it as an adjunct to other information. Nevertheless, the score can be a decisive factor in determining the type of loan package for which you are eligible.

THE KEY ELEMENTS OF CREDIT SCORING

The complex formula for scoring assigns the greatest weight to the absence of problems, then brings your score down according to what problem or condition is noted and how old it is. In other words, you don't want to be a "credit lightweight" by having your record peppered with flaws. Some of the problems and conditions that reduce your score are as follows, according to the Beacon system.

It is important to note that they do not impact your score equally.

- Current outstanding balances on accounts
- Not all accounts paid as agreed
- Too few bank or national revolving/open accounts. No bank or revolving/open accounts would certainly qualify as "too few"
- Number of accounts with outstanding balances
- Number of finance company accounts
- Recent payment history is too new to rate
- Number of inquiries within the last 12 months
- Number of accounts opened within the last 12 months
- Relationship of balance to high credit on bank/national or other revolving/open accounts
- Outstanding balances on revolving/open accounts
- Length of time revolving/open accounts have been established
- Length of time (or unknown time) since account not paid as agreed or trade narrative reported
- Length of time accounts have been established
- Lack of recent information on bank or national accounts, or lack of bank or national accounts
- Lack of recent information revolving/open accounts, or lack of revolving/open accounts
- No non-mortgage account balances, or non-mortgage balances not recently reported
- Number of accounts currently or in the past not paid as agreed
- Too few accounts currently paid as agreed
- Length of time since public record or collection agency filing
- Amount past due on accounts
- Account not paid as agreed, public record, or collection agency filing

- Too many bank or national revolving/open accounts with outstanding balances

- Lack of recently reported balances on revolving/open accounts

Since the number of inquiries affects your score, you should ensure that every company listed as inquiring about your credit has been authorized by you to do so. Any company that obtains your credit information without your authorization has violated federal law. Your authorization flows from sources such as applications for a credit card, job, or loan.

TRUE STORY: UNAUTHORIZED CREDIT INQUIRY

The journalist who published a scathing investigative report about the Church of Scientology in the May 6, 1991, issue of Time magazine alleged that harassment by Scientologists included illegal retrieval of his credit report. He stated that the report went to a "sham company" called Educational Funding Services of Los Angeles, which gave as its address a mail drop near Scientology's headquarters. According to the reporter, a private investigator admitted to him that a security official for the church retained him to retrieve credit reports on several people. The premise was that Scientology attorneys had judgments against the individuals and wanted to collect amounts owed.

The main elements of scoring are tied to three questions:

1. How bad are the problems?

2. How recent are the problems?

3. How many problems are there?

If you look at your credit report and can honestly say, "There are a couple things here and there, but my record over the past two years looks darn good," then your score will probably be high. If you have a lot of revolving debt, however, even if your record is spotless, your score will be low. Also, if you know there are errors on your credit report, your score will reflect the incorrect information until it is removed.

TRUE STORY: COSTLY CREDIT SCORING MISTAKES

Steve Johns worked at a credit reporting agency and his wife was a certified public accountant. Steve had spent years saving, using credit cautiously, and compulsively paying his bills on time. His wife was exactly the same way. At one point, he had the privilege of seeing his credit score: 780 out of a possible 900. Even though he is one of few people in the country who can claim to be so saintly in his financial standing, he was disappointed. Where did he lose 120 points?

The source was a mistake on the credit report. He and his wife were, in fact, a perfect credit couple.

THE IMPORTANCE OF CREDIT SCORING TO A LENDER

The point of scoring is to aid a credit grantor with risk assessment, not to calculate a debt ratio. This is one reason why certain actions you would take to improve your position with a lender may have no impact or even negative impact on your credit score. For example, reducing your account balances or closing accounts may not improve your score because the use and mix of available credit could be upset. It might actually lower your score while it dramatically improves your debt-to-income ratio! In the mortgage process, the lender is far more concerned about that ratio in deciding whether or not to do business with you. Whether or not you qualify for an optimum loan package, however, may be tied to your score.

Here is one example of how the score could affect your mortgage. A November 20, 1995, rate sheet from one bank in California offered an introductory interest rate of 7.25 percent for the first three months of the loan to borrowers with a Fair Isaac Company (FICO) score of at least 640. After the initial period, the rate increased by .50 percent for borrowers of $50,000 with a 680 score and by 1.00 percent for borrowers of $200,000 with a 680 score. Borrowers of $50,000 with a 640 score, however, would see a rate increase of 1.00 percent; those with $200,000 loans would pay an additional 1.75 percent. The bank also offered a package for financing a second home to the 680-and-above scorers, but offered no package at all to those who scored 640 or below.

The difference in monthly payments (allowing reasonable amounts for taxes and hazard insurance) after the initial three-month period would be as follows:

	Borrower with 680 score	*Borrower with 640 score*
$ 50,000	$ 430.70	$ 448.13
$200,000	$1,792.53	$1,899.24

Total payments of about $176,000 *versus* $183,000 for a $50,000 loan, and about $732,000 *versus* $770,000 for a $200,000 loan. What a significant difference in options, influenced by something as seemingly minor as one-too-many inquiries about your credit!

If you keep your credit record clean and accurate, your score should be good enough to give you a boost with a lender. If your score isn't great, you may find that American Express and VISA Gold don't want you, but plenty of lenders may, depending on what else is in your portfolio. However, once you receive your credit score, there is no immediate way to improve it.

As you'll see in a moment, those other items go beyond the credit report and scores in helping you prove that you should get the mortgage and the house of your dreams.

Chapter 4

Gaining Speed: Create More Financial Leverage

A credit history is just that—history. Unfortunately, most lenders have a nagging focus on the past, and use every flaw in your credit record as justification for punishing you with rejection or high borrowing rates. Seven years without a possibility of "parole" for a 30-day late notation is a stiff sentence! One of the potential buyer's greatest challenges may be convincing the lender that the past does not equal the future and that one-time poor financial management or a trauma like sudden job loss has not set the pace for the rest of your financial life

How do you create more financial leverage from the present and the future than from the past? Nontraditional credit records, sources of income and assets, and image-boosting actions will make you more appealing to a lender. You may be surprised at the impact a little bit of debt reduction has on borrowing power.

Keep in mind that one single item will not sway a lender. But the combination of mutually reinforcing facts will help you qualify for the loan of your choice.

POWERING UP YOUR CREDIT HISTORY

You're probably tired of reading about the ways the lending system works against you, so here is a chapter devoted to creative and nontraditional ways to make it work for you.

Trade accounts and other debt items covered in your credit report figure into your *debt-to-income ratio*. This is the relationship of debt to income that lenders review to make an initial assessment of your capacity to handle mortgage debt. Telephone and utility payments do not appear on your credit report and do not affect your debt-to-income ratio. They can, however, have a positive impact on your credit picture by demonstrating your ability to pay on time.

For example, Pacific Gas & Electric Company (PG&E) in California provides a statement to good customers that says, in effect, "Over the past year, you have paid us on time. You may use this letter as proof of that fact." Similarly, Kaiser Permanente adds a tag line to certain statements that says, "Thank you for consistently paying your account on time." Consider every paper like this a legitimate credit document, and introduce it into your mortgage package if you need evidence that your recent payment patterns show a marked improvement over your history.

Several non-bureau sources of credit information can indicate you are a steady bill-payer and/or a careful planner.

Telephone bills. Your phone bills not only document on-time paying, but serve as evidence that a deposit on new service has been waived due to a strong record with the service provider.

Utility bills. As noted in the PG&E example, your utility company may automatically provide you with a favorable statement of your payment record. If not, the bill itself is proof that your payments have been made in a timely fashion if there is no "past due amount" listed on it.

Canceled Checks to Landlord. Unless your landlord behaves uncharacteristically and delays depositing your on-time payment for days or weeks, your canceled rent checks provide critical evidence to a lender that "housing comes first." Include 12 months of checks in your mortgage package.

Insurance Payments. The example of Kaiser's automatic statement is just one of many types of credit support you may have in your drawer. Think of all the insurance payments that a family can have: health, life, property, automobile, and more.

Authorized User on Someone Else's Account. Canceled checks providing evidence that you paid the bills on time will count in your favor, no matter whose credit was used to secure the account. Note well, however, that once you bring the debt into your credit picture, it will affect the calculation of your debt-to-income ratio.

Medical Bills. A cumulative statement from your dentist might read as follows:

5/22	Periodic Exam	$39
5/22	Payment-Thank You	($39)
7/20	Periodontal Maintenance	$97
7/20	Payment-Thank You	($97)
8/18	Emergency Visit-Repair Crown	$300
8/18	Payment-Thank You	($100)
9/1	Payment-Thank You	($100)
9/15	Payment-Thank You	($100)

This may not seem impressive, but statements like this illustrate your ability to meet on-going, as well as unexpected, obligations while keeping a roof over your head. If you have a bumpy credit record, this is evidence that you are now driving on a well-paved road.

Other Monthly Obligations Not Reflected on Your Credit Report. You may be a business owner who has accounts at office supply stores, or with warehouses or temporary agencies: Use the evidence at hand to create a complete picture of your creditworthiness.

 If you have any accounts paid through automatic withdrawals from a bank account or automatic charges to a credit card, your records of payment with them should be flawless. Use statements documenting that fact in your loan package as proof of your reliability. A letter from a credit grantor stating that you have paid "as agreed" for a number of months or years is a particularly powerful tool.

TRUE STORY: CREDIT HISTORY WITHOUT CREDIT BUREAUS

Sergio Mangera owned a thriving restaurant in Arlington, Virginia, but he had never bothered to establish credit card accounts and had paid for his car in cash. After being in the country for five years, he was still a "non-person" in the eyes of creditors. To them, he might as well have still been in Brazil! When he wanted to buy a house, he was

laughed out of the bank, even with a 20 percent down payment on the property and strong cash reserves. How could
Sergio's risk factors be evaluated when there was no record
of him at TRW, Equifax or Trans Union?

A mortgage broker devised a plan that worked. He had
Sergio get a verification of rent and compile statements
from the produce, meat and liquor suppliers that showed his
accounts were always paid on time. He added to that similar
statements from the laundry that did Sergio's tablecloths,
the company that picked up his garbage, and the service that
cleaned and maintained the restaurant space. By the time
Sergio's pile of nontraditional credit documentation was
complete, a large bank not only agreed to do business with
him, but also offered him a favorable deal.

When providing supplements to credit reports, borrower's credit
explanations, written explanation of employment or employment gap, and any other letters or key documents, lenders want
originals, but to expedite the process, they will accept faxed
copies to be signed later.

POWERING UP YOUR CAPACITY

One of the primary points of this chapter is that your capacity to
absorb a mortgage into your debt structure is not as strictly quanti-
tative as some lenders would have you believe. For example, you may
be making $40,000 annually as a nurse now, but have a five-year
union contract with a guaranteed cost of living increase plus 1% a
year. This is a compelling statement of your future capacity.

TRUE STORY: MUSIC CONTRACTS POWER UP CAPACITY

Darryl Powers was a percussionist with the National
Symphony. On the side, he also performed with a jazz band.
Per his union contract, his base salary with the Symphony
was $65,000, with yearly incremental increases; he also had
a tidy income playing at the clubs. When his club gigs led to

a recording contract, he then had two documents stating his "guaranteed" income that your and the coming year. I he lender decided the evidence was powerful enough to look past the less-than-ideal ratio and proceed with the loan.

Similarly, a written letter of intent to seek employment for a spouse may be considered. This is especially relevant in the event of a relocation related to one spouse's job, when the other one had been working. (See the discussion below of *trailing spouse income*, a potentially major factor in demonstrating capacity.) It could also apply if a spouse has recently finished a training and/or academic program. Evidence of marketability, such as a diploma, can help bolster the case.

Review the following non-salary sources of income and see if they might be added to your financial picture in the upcoming months:

Retirement Income. Perhaps you are recently retired from military service, have a new civilian job, and anticipate steady retirement income with cost-of-living increases, contingent on acts of Congress. Tell the lender because this could make a sizable difference. (Although, could you blame a lender for questioning anything reliant on acts of Congress?)

If you are already receiving a pension, you'll most likely want to include it on your loan application under "Other Income." Tax-free income can have more impact than face value, because many lenders will "gross it up," or adjust it upward, to acknowledge the fact that nothing is deducted from it. This makes sense if you consider that your taxable income is reviewed on a gross-basis, rather than after taxes have been deducted.

Trailing Spouse Income. Lenders will usually give special consideration to a two-income couple that has temporarily become a one-income couple because of a relocation related to career advancement. In calculating ratios, you would use a combination of the relocated spouse's current income plus the "trailing spouse's" most recent income. Attach a letter of intent to seek work for the trailing spouse when you submit verification of the previous income.

Gifts. You may have a parent, sibling or other blood relative in a position to give you a portion of your down payment, but there are cautions associated with a *gift*. Lenders want borrowers to contribute at least 5 percent of the purchase price from their own funds. This minimum contribution must be used as down payment. Therefore, if the intent is to make a 15 percent down payment, the gift letter should indicate that a certain amount of the gift is meant for closing costs, so it is clear that your 5-percent is earmarked for the down payment.

A gift letter must clearly state that: 1) There is no expectation of repayment, and 2) precisely what the giver's relationship is to the recipient. It must also have attached to it one month's bank statement verifying that the donor has the ability to give. This documentation may seem excessive, but lenders do not want to have borrowers, especially those with high ratios and/or high loan-to-value (LTV), qualifying for a loan with a "gift" that is really another loan.

TRUE STORY: FINDING CASH

Clem and Sissy Barlow had a combined income of $60,000 and had saved $10,000 for a down payment—quite short of the 10% down payment on their desired property with a sales price of $131,500, not to mention closing costs, impounds for taxes, insurance and mortgage insurance, and cash reserves of 2–3 months PITI. Clem and Sissy made a counter offer of $128,500. They were lucky: The seller needed to move and was willing to come down in price if the deal could be made immediately. Where could they find the extra cash they needed?

In reviewing their assets, their broker noticed a retirement account of $7,000, which helped, but was not enough to pull them into the target range for available cash once they paid all the penalties and taxes linked to early withdrawal of the funds.

Sissy's brother decided to give them a wedding present he couldn't afford four years prior. He gave them a check for

$2500, along with a gift letter and bank statement to add to their package.

Although Clem and Sissy then had a total of $16,500, they were slightly short of the mark. Annoying, yet necessary, charges like title and escrow fees, appraisal costs, credit report, and applications fees would strain them unless they could find another $1,000. Sissy decided to take the equity she had in a life insurance policy her father established for her when she was born.

Are all these actions wise choices? Not necessarily, but you should know what options are available and how they can sway a lender to say, "Yes."

Social Security Income. Again, if you expect social security income in the near future that will supplement the income you listed on your loan application, you should indicate that to the lender. This will require an awards letter from the Social Security Administration; it comes in advance of your first payment. You may find repeated need for this letter, so protect it.

Unemployment Compensation. Depending on your career field, unemployment payments may play a regular role in your finances.

TRUE STORY: SHOWING UNEMPLOYMENT INCOME

Like Darryl Powers, Lainie Marma was a percussionist, but she was only employed seasonally with an orchestra, so she didn't have the same level of job security. She owned a place in Jamaica, as well as a home in New Orleans. When rates dropped and she tried to refinance the New Orleans property, lenders told her she did not make enough to qualify. One thing finally pushed her income into the acceptable range: She documented through tax returns that every year for the past 3 years, she received unemployment compensation amounting to $6,000 yearly due to the lack of openings for percussionists.

Child support, Alimony, and/or Separate Maintenance Payments. If you are a newly single parent trying to buy a house, and your divorce or separation agreement indicates that you are to receive payments, include the agreement in your mortgage package. And if you have received payments as agreed, include evidence of that through a bank statement or copies of checks.

Notes Receivable. Does anyone owe you money, and is it formally documented? Are you an entrepreneur who completed contracts that are, as yet, unpaid, but have a positive history of doing business with the person or company? Although these sources of income are not continuing and ongoing, they can be used as compensating factors. A lender might consider them important if your available cash after closing looks marginal.

Trust Income. You should know if you're about to gain access to a trust fund. If so, this can create powerful financial leverage and should be noted in you loan package through a copy of the trust agreement.

VA Benefits. It can take months or years to get the Veterans Administration to process the paperwork required to secure disability benefits, but if your request has been properly endorsed, you have a reasonable expectation of receiving from about $100 to well over $1,000 a month in tax-free assistance. Use your awards letter to document this income stream.

Similarly, if you qualify for veterans' educational benefits, you have a tax-free supplemental income for a period of time that is very predictable. Whether or not that income affects your borrowing status, however, depends partially on your circumstances, and partially on the lender. In order to accept such income in calculating ratios, most lenders want to see a 2-year history of receipt, plus a 3-year probability of continuance. If you have a less than a 3-year future with the income source, but are in a field like medicine or computer science, where a degree almost certainly means a job, then the lender might bend.

POWERING UP YOUR CHARACTER

The character criterion becomes important for a lender when the prospective borrower has experienced a bankruptcy, series of judgments, or other financial crises. A lender will not disregard history even if you have "reformed," but may consider evidence of that reform compelling enough to approve a loan. Similarly, if your ratios are above the allowable limits, *compensating factors* related to your character can move the ceiling upward. These factors are like grains of sand on a scale. One grain doesn't make a discernible difference, but a dozen do.

It is you, the borrower, who must force the lender to focus on your reliability and consistency through impressive documentation. It is up to you to ensure that the lender feels the weight of the sand.

Regardless of your situation, you can establish your good character through the following means, and more:

- Automatic savings deductions from payroll.

- Regular contributions to your retirement fund.

- Investment in certificates of deposits, Series E bonds, or other savings programs for your children's education.

- Maintenance of a term or whole life insurance policy, that will result in a cash payment to you when mature or a face-value payment to your heirs in the event of your premature death.

Depending on your field of study, academic credentials can also advance your case with a lender. Completion of medical, law school, or business school and the associated internships is an accomplishment signaling potentially high earnings to a lender. You may make the case that it applies in other fields, too, depending on your geographic location. You can obviously build a stronger case if you have also received a job offer in writing from a practice or hospital, research facility, corporation, law firm, brokerage house or other employer in your credentialed field.

Now, with your fresh perspective on your creditworthiness, you are ready to choose a loan.

Chapter 5

The First Big Intersection: Select a Mortgage Type

Your first big intersection in the Mortgage Maze is understanding the types of different loans available, and how to match your situation to the right mortgage. If you start with the right questions, you will move logically toward the best loan product for you.

Exercises with QualifyR will illustrate how payment amounts and requirements vary among loan types. By the end of the chapter, you will feel secure in telling your loan originator which options you want to explore, and which you want to disregard.

THE FIRST STEP TO LOAN SELECTION: PERSONAL CHOICE

Many people who have refinanced or purchased homes three or four times know almost nothing about selecting a mortgage. This is particularly common with successful professionals who invest in property beyond the roof over their head. Their mortgage brokers or advisors don't bother to explain loan terms to them either because they assume a level of existing knowledge, or they assume the client doesn't want to be bothered with the details. This lack of knowledge begins the fast track to financial ruin.

Some loan officers are either so green or so averse to customer service, that they can't or won't explain the details of different loan products. They see their sole job as overcoming objections to the product they are pushing on you (that is, the one that earns them the most money). On the good side, you may be able to use the loan officer's strong motivation to close a deal by *locking in* a good rate early in the process. Most people have quite a different experience with these loan officers, however. If you have no objections or questions, you learn nothing about the relative advantages of one loan package over another. Even if you have objections, there is no guarantee you will get an education in the loan process that can help you make sound choices.

Whether you decide to go it alone in navigating the Mortgage Maze or secure the help of a professional mortgage broker and/or a loan agent at a bank or other lending institution, you need to begin the process of selecting your loan type with the right question. After that, it's a matter of deductive reasoning.

The right question is one that first compels you to examine yourself and then guides you toward matching your situation and preferences with the economy. Because economic factors can profoundly influence what loan type is best for you, don't be surprised if you find yourself changing your mind as you go through the loan selection steps in this chapter. The only constant in the Mortgage Maze is change.

MATCHING LOAN TYPE TO RISK TOLERANCE

Starting with "How much can I spend?," or "What can I afford?," is necessary for prequalification, but when it comes to selecting a loan product, the question is not a good starter. It immediately places restrictions on your leverage and makes you vulnerable. You wouldn't initiate a car purchase by marching into a showroom and declaring, "I can spend $300 a month. What should I buy?" So don't begin shopping for a mortgage with a similar approach. "What will my bank offer me?" is another one that places you at the mercy and kind nature of a loan officer. Good luck with that. You need to know what you'll accept rather than what a lender will offer.

The logical place to start is by questioning your tolerance for risk. How much unpredictability in your mortgage payment can you handle comfortably? And if you take a risk, what is the potential reward? In asking yourself, "What is my tolerance for risk?" you are questioning both your financial and your psychological capacity to deal with varying payments. An integral part of the answer is an explanation of the basic types of loans: fixed-rate mortgage, adjustable rate mortgage (ARM), *two-step mortgage* (*Fixed interim-rate mortgage or FIRM*), and a *fixed balloon note*.

Take a quick look at the Compare module in QualifyR. Although the display of loan types will make more sense later, it is a good overview of possibilities as you begin to examine these loan types.

The FIRM with a low start, fixed for 5–7 years, with a one-time adjustment to another fixed rate for the life of a 30-year loan, which is either 25 or 23 years respectively from Fannie Mae and Freddie Mac, may include terms that allow the lender to transform the loan into a balloon note. When you take 5/25 or 7/23 *conforming loan* (a loan no greater than $207,000), you sign a balloon-note rate rider that spells out the 5 conditions under which your loan is due and payable after your first fixed period.

FIXED-RATE MORTGAGE

With a fixed-rate mortgage, the interest rate is fixed for the life of the loan and the debt is *amortized*, or paid in equal monthly installments. It has a steady, flat payment with no change. Whether that life, or amortization period, is 30 years, 15 years, or even less, the payments remain constant until the balance is zero.

This is the loan for someone with no tolerance for movement in the interest rate, someone who invests in government bonds rather than volatile stocks and new ventures, someone who does not want to review the money rate section of the *Wall Street Journal* daily to figure out what the next mortgage payment will be. If you have a fixed income, or one that does not move with the economy, this is your loan. Or if you are merely conservative by nature, this is your loan.

A fixed-rate loan is predictable. You have certainty that as the years go by, you will never have payment shock. What you paid in the first month of your home ownership is that same amount you will pay when you're old and gray and the roof on your house has been replaced once or twice.

With either a fixed- or adjustable-rate mortgage, the greatest portion of your payment applies to interest for about the first 17 years of a 30-year amortization period, unless you develop the capacity to make extra payments periodically. If your payments are fixed while your income rises, you can easily budget for an occasional extra payment, which is applied directly to principal. This increases your equity and decreases the life of the loan.

Another advantage to the fixed rate is that after some years, you'll also feel smug for having a better deal than anyone else on the block. And finally, virtually all large lenders offer fixed-rate mortgages.

One disadvantage to the fixed-rate loan is no *introductory rate*, or *teaser rate* which is a lower interest rate at the outset of a loan that helps you qualify for a larger amount. Your monthly obligation will be constant from Day 1 to Day 10,950.

Secondly, in some years, you later may kick yourself for being locked into a rate that's comparatively high. Of course, if you kick yourself hard enough you'll refinance since that's the only way to reduce your monthly payment. Principal reductions through extra payments shorten the amortization period, but don't lower the payment amount.

ARM (ADJUSTABLE RATE MORTGAGE)

With an adjustable-rate mortgage (ARM), the interest rate is adjusted periodically to keep it consonant with changing market rates. It has the lowest start interest rate, the easiest qualifying, and is usually predictable early, but not always. Bankers like this because the loan stays close to their cost of funds, a phenomenon referred to as *marking to market*. This allows banks or institutions the ability to match their assets to their liabilities.

The ARM is the loan for a good planner who has alternative sources of funds or disposable assets. Handling an adjustable-rate mortgage is really a cash-flow issue, so entrepreneurs who are adept at dealing with the cash fluctuations in a business are often well-suited for the ARM. Also, it is a good loan for you if you expect

windfall profits that will allow you to reduce the principal substan
tially, thereby lowering your monthly debt.

ARMs involve a teaser rate so the initial payments are lower. This
introductory rate is arbitrary, set by the lender to lure you into a
deal. Another advantage is that the ARM adjusts to the then-current
balance, and one of the factors that influences the size of your payment is the ever-decreasing balance for which the interest is charged.

Extra payments reduce the life of a fixed-rate mortgage. This
means they shorten the amortization period. Extra payments do
not affect the amortization period of an ARM. Extra payments
reduce the size of payments of an ARM because they reduce the
principal balance on which the interest is calculated.

Another benefit is that ARMs afford you the highest degree of
control. They enable you to manage your cash flow by making the
minimum payments (PITI) when necessary, and to reduce principal
on an accelerated basis without *prepayment penalty* (*PPP*).

A prepayment penalty period is normally the first 3 to 5 years of
the loan. Any loan that has a PPP allows you to reduce the balance each of those years by up to, but never exceeding, 20 percent
without PPP. The amount of PPP varies, but would look something like this for a 3-year PPP period: 3 percent of 80 percent of
the principal balance for paying off the loan in the first year;
2 percent of 80 percent of the balance for paying it off in the second year; and 1 percent of 80 percent of the balance for paying it
off in the final year.

In general, ARMs allow you to qualify for a higher loan amount.
If you are in the early years of your career, an ARM may be the best
route to your dream house. Or there may be times of low interest
rates when you feel as if you've gotten a healthy bonus. And, if you
are a good planner, that "bonus" should allow you to handle the
upward shifts in interest with ease, or to add to your payment amount
to reduce the principal balance. Adding $100 to the minimum to

reduce your balance is like a $100 gift to yourself in the sense that you are no longer paying interest on that money. The catch, of course, is that the cash is no longer available to you.

There are negative aspects to the ARM. Your payment amount could kill your vacation plans or force you to live on macaroni and cheese if interest rates skyrocket. So, although there is a cap on how much your rate can fluctuate, you may still feel financially depleted for many months at a time.

With an ARM, there are key variables that influence the pros and cons, such as which *index* is used to establish rate changes, the percent of *margin* used to calculate the rate, the length of the adjustment period, caps on interest rate or payments, and more.

The index plus the margin equals the *fully indexed* interest rate. The margin is constant for the life of your loan; the index is an economic indicator that moves with the economy. So, for example, if the current index value is 6.5 percent and the margin is 2 percent, the fully indexed rate is 8.5 percent.

Different indexes may be used in the calculation: The index used can make an enormous difference in the desirability of the loan. The following chart illustrates differences between the London Interbank Offering Rate (LIBOR) and the 2.75 percent (average) margin associated with it, for example, and the Federal Home Loan Bank (FHLB) 11th District Cost of Funds Index (COFI, pronounced "coffee") with its associated 2.4 percent margin. For the period January 1, 1993 and ending December 31, 1994, with a monthly adjustment:

LIBOR high rate:	6.141+2.75 margin=8.891 fully indexed rate
LIBOR low rate:	3.141+2.75 margin=5.891 fully indexed rate
	Variance: 3.00
COFI high rate:	4.589+2.4 margin=6.989 fully indexed rate
COFI low rate:	3.629+2.4 margin=6.029 fully indexed rate
	Variance: .96

The variance of .96 percent seems insignificant, but it amounts to $960 for the year on a loan balance of $100,000.

The 11th District is an actual geographic region composed of Arizona, California and Nevada. The *cost of funds* means, literally, what the cost of money is for the savings and loan associations and savings banks in that area. That cost is determined by establishing a weighted average interest rate on money that the institutions owe to any source of its funds. Similarly, the LIBOR index reflects the cost to 5 large European banks of maintaining their dollar accounts.

It is logical that lenders would tie the price of a mortgage to their cost of funds. If they are ever going to make money, they need to charge more for lending than they pay for borrowing. Perhaps the surprising thing is the profit margin is so low. If a bank makes 1 percent profit on the funds that flow in and out of its vaults, the bank is considered very successful. (Unless, of course, a felonious act siphons off the earnings through investment in get-rich-quick schemes like junk bonds or derivatives.)

In addition to LIBOR and COFI, other popular indexes are 6-month United States Treasury Bills; 1-year U.S. Treasury Securities, or to use the proper name, the "yield on United States Treasury Securities adjusted to a constant maturity of 1 year"; 3-year U.S. Treasury Securities; and the "final national average contract interest rate on the purchase of previously-occupied single-family homes."

Indexes are different in another way, too: They can be weighted average or spot indexes. COFI is a *weighted index*, so its movement with the economy on a monthly basis affects your interest rate, and payment size, on a monthly basis. In contrast, some ARMs are calculated using a *spot index*. The preset formula might be that 45 days before your annual adjustment date, the 1-year U.S. Treasury rate on that particular day (plus the margin) dictates your rate for the next year. If the rate on that day sat at 4.53, for example, with a 2.75 margin, your rate for the year would be 7.28. That could be a lucky break, or it could break your heart depending on how the economy moves. In a way, using a spot index is like a roll of the dice!

CAUTION

Treasury Security indices have both a weekly and a monthly value. In the course of examining the merits of a loan package, you should make sure the lender specifies which one is being used for your ARM, and be sure the calculations reflect the correct one. Lenders commonly make calculation errors because they use the wrong index. It is not a malicious act, it's just a mistake that can be avoided if the lender does not rush through the calculation.

The next major consideration in a fully amortizing ARM is your adjustment period, which could be semi-annually, yearly, or some other period. If your fully indexed start rate is 5.5 percent, your rate cap per annual adjustment period is 2 percent, and you have a life-time cap of 6 percent, your lifetime ceiling rate is 11.5 percent. That shift from 5.5 percent to 11.5 percent could be devastating, however, if it occurs consistently during a time when you don't have the capacity to deal with escalating monthly payments. You might also have a floor rate that would ensure you never pay less than 6 percent interest.

Using these sample numbers, here is a worst-case scenario illustrating how your payments might escalate on a $100,000 loan with an interest-rate adjustment cap. This example uses a one-year adjustment period, such as the kind that might be associated with the 1-year U.S. Treasury Security index.

Worst-Case ARM Scenario

Year	1	2	3	4
Percent Adj.	5.5	7.5	9.5	11.5 (cap)
Mo. Payment	$567.79	$696.21	$831.98	$973.15
Percent Change		22.62	19.50	16.97
Overall Payment Differential				58.35 percent

Fortunately, a more likely progression would be movement with a fully indexed rate. You would start with a rate of 5.5; if the 1-year Treasury Security index were at 4, adding to that a 2.75 margin would give you a second-year rate of 6.75, rather than 7.5, percent.

FIRM (Two-Step Mortgage)

A FIRM meaning "Fixed-interim-rate mortgage" is a two-step mortgage. Two types of FIRM are available: 1) low start, fixed for 5 or 7 years, with a one-time adjustment to another fixed rate for the life of the loan, or 2) low start, fixed for 3, 5, 7, or 10 years, that rolls into an adjustable-rate mortgage with interest or payment caps for the duration.

A two-step, or FIRM, mortgage involves a rate adjustment after an initial period. That change can be to either of the following: 1) another fixed rate based on a predetermined schedule of principal and interest, as well as predetermined conditions, or 2) an adjustable rate-mortgage. Under certain conditions, the first type is a balloon loan that will be called due by the lender.

If you ask a dozen different loan officers to explain the conditions and terms of a conforming 5/25 or 7/23, you will get a dozen different answers. Be careful with this one: There are great advantages and potentially huge pitfalls to a confirming FIRM from Fannie Mae or Freddie Mac.

The FIRM is a loan for the strong of heart, someone who is an excellent planner. A one-time adjustment to the then-current rate that lasts for the next 23 or 25 years, can throw you into financial turmoil if any aspect of your projections goes awry.

Pros and Cons of the FIRM. As with the traditional ARM, a lower introductory rate protects you from major rate fluctuations in the early years of ownership or refinancing, and may help you qualify for a bigger loan amount and enhance financial stability. This loan can be the best choice if you know you will be moving and selling the house or repaying the loan at the end of the initial period of 5 or 7 years.

The FIRM can also be the best choice if you plan to remodel a home to a dramatic extent; this increases the loan-to-value ratio substantially. In other words, if you put 20 percent down on a $100,000 house, then increase the value of the house by $20,000, you own 20 percent of a more valuable house. A definite plan to refinance, due to an impending promotion, in which income is going to increase substantially, or the addition of a family member, can also make a FIRM an attractive option.

A family member graduating from college or rejoining the work force would release more cash into the family coffers and would create a situation that would also make this loan desirable. A fundamental advantage is that a 5-year FIRM carries a rate of approximately .5 percent less than a 30-year fixed rate; a 7-year FIRM is about .375 less than a 30-year fixed.

There are some cons to choosing the FIRM. At the end of the initial period of 5 or 7 years, it is possible to get payment shock. If plans to move or repay fall through, you could be stuck with an undesirable rate for the life of the loan, or worse yet, be forced to refinance to pay off the existing loan.

Another disadvantage is that this loan is marked to market without limitation in some cases. If the rate moves 5 percent or more upward, the lender may be able to call the loan due, that is, make it a balloon note. You are stuck if you are not able to qualify for the same loan amount due to changes in your financial health or rates that escalate 5 percent or more.

FIXED BALLOON NOTE

The fixed balloon note starts with a low interest rate for a period of time that rolls into a no-option, dead-end situation. You must pay off the loan at the point the balloon is due. A balloon note, which involves a lump-sum payment after a certain number of years of small payments, is almost never a smart choice.

In the Maze Master's opinion . . .
Balloons explode. Don't buy them.

With a *balloon note,* your periodic payments are low because they are based on a longer amortization period. That doesn't mean you have a longer time to pay, just that your payments are based on a longer period. The overpayment amount allows you to qualify for more house, but in order for the loan to be fully amortized loan, a principal sum called a "balloon" must be paid at maturity. This loan is for you if you have unshakable faith that an investment you made will pay off, or if you have good reason to believe that your income will rise dramatically.

The fundamental principle of real estate planning always includes a plan for the worst case situation. This idiom applies no matter how conservative or how risk-oriented your mortgage is. If you are adept at crisis planning, even with a balloon note, you will be fine.

With a balloon note, one advantage is that you will have comparatively or predictably small payments for an extended period of time, without any movement whatsoever. On the other hand, eventually you will face a gigantic payment if all the conditions of adjustment are not met. In the meantime, you have built up very little equity.

And, if you get caught having to refinance, you will again have to pay all the costs, emotional and financial, associated with the mortgage process.

Your personal and financial picture may allow you to choose from these four loan types. However, as we pointed out in the beginning, the risk varies greatly among them. To ascertain your tolerance for risk, ask yourself these questions. Give yourself, or yourself and your co-borrower, 0 points for every no," 1 point for every "it's possible," and 2 points for every "yes."

1. Are you established in a job and likely to see a sizable salary increase soon?

2. Whether or not you are established in a job, do you have a sense that your income over the next few years will increase at least as much as the economy?

3. Do you expect a windfall that might allow you to pay the remaining balance on a home loan?

4. Is it unlikely your family will increase in size, whether it's a baby or a grandparent?

5. Are you a good saver, regularly putting 10 percent of your earnings in reserve?

6. Are you comfortable with changes in your debt, from something as minor as replacing a TV to a major one like a new car purchase?

7. Can you think of several non-salary sources of funds you can access quickly?

The closer to "14" you scored, the higher your tolerance for risk, and *vice versa*.

MATCHING LOAN TYPE TO TIMELINE

Now you should have some sense of the kind of borrower you are in terms of risk—low (fixed), medium (certain types of ARMs and FIRMS), or high (other ARMs and balloons). Your next question relates to the amount of time you choose to carry the mortgage debt.

If you are a low-risk person with strong capacity, you may want to take on a 15 or 10 year fixed-rate mortgage, rather than a 30-year term. Some good reasons to shorten the time are getting a better rate, building more equity rapidly, and for retirement planning purposes.

Regarding retirement planning, your last years of working should be your highest income years in which you will need strong tax advantages, but after which your house payments should still be manageable.

If you can secure a 30-year loan at 7.5 percent, you might be able to get a 15-year loan at 7 percent, and a 10-year at 6.75 percent. On a $100,000 loan, the difference in monthly payments of principal and interest, and balances at 5-year increments, would be as follows:

	Payment	Balance after 5 Yrs	10 Yrs
30-year @ 7.5%:	$ 699.21	$94,617.44	$86,794.99
15-year @ 7%:	$ 898.83	$77,412.80	$45,392.62
10-year @ 6.75%:	$1,148.24	$58,335.33	-0-

 Here is where you can begin using the QualifyR software, as well as World Wide Web sites, to compare the effect of different amortization periods on your own situation. If you use QualifyR, go to the Estimate module and insert your figures; be sure to list "mortgage type" as "30 Yr Fixed/Conventional." Then, go to the Compare module and view the differences in interest rates and payments of the 30, 20, 15 and 10 year periods. Note how dramatically your monthly income requirement jumps when you cut the amortization period in half or to one-third!

If you use Web sites such as HSH Associates (www.hsh.com) or www.maze.com, you have the advantage of being able to compare current interest rates for the different loans.

Clearly, if you expect an increase in income in the near future, see if you qualify for a loan with a shorter term than the standard 30 years.

If you are a medium risk person, consider that your situation may drive you toward a FIRM rather than a straight ARM. If you are a presidential appointee during the second term of a presidency, for example, you have a good sense of when your job in Washington, DC will end. You may be well-suited for a loan with a low initial rate that rolls into a long-term fixed or into an adjustable rate, since you fully expect to be out of town with your property sold by the time the rollover would have to take place. But what if your property doesn't sell that easily?

The following contrast between a 3-year fixed/27-year ARM (FIRM) and a fixed-rate mortgage shows how the shifting rate can turn against borrowers when they don't stick to their timeline. In this example, the purchaser chose a FIRM instead of a fixed rate mortgage because he expected to be transferred in 3 years and sell the house. He did not sell the house until the fifth year and suffered the consequences financially:

FIRM	Fixed
3-year fixed/27-year ARM	30-year fixed rate
7.125% first 3 years; 2% maximum interest rate cap per year, next 27 years	7.75% for 30 years
Total savings after 3 years: 1.875% (.625 × 3)	(Loss) after 3 years: (1.875%)
4th year interest rate: 9.125%	4th year savings: 1.375%
5th year interest rate: 11.125%	5th year savings: 3.375%
Net (loss) after 5 years: (2.875%)	Net savings after 5 years: 2.875%

If the borrower had sold in 3 years as originally planned, the savings would be 1.875% over the fixed rate. When the house was not sold until after 5 years, he lost the three-year savings and paid another 2.875% more than the fixed rate loan. (This example maximized the annual interest cap on the ARM.) Nevertheless, the FIRM still makes sense for someone starting a new job who is in transition professionally, with the likelihood of promotion and raise accompanying that transition.

Another product that builds on the x years fixed/ARM, is a loan with a convertible option, almost always part of a 3/ARM. At a stated window, perhaps 24th to 60th months, you would have the option of converting a 3/ARM to a fixed-rate loan for the duration of the amortization period. The conversion is based on the then-current Fannie Mae 60-day rate plus .625 for conforming and .875 for jumbo (over $207,000 in most locations) or a percentage of the Fannie Mae 60-day rate plus margin. These margins may change up or down depending on your lender.

 By building on your comparison of amortization periods for fixed rate loans, you can now add various ARMS to the mix using QualifyR.

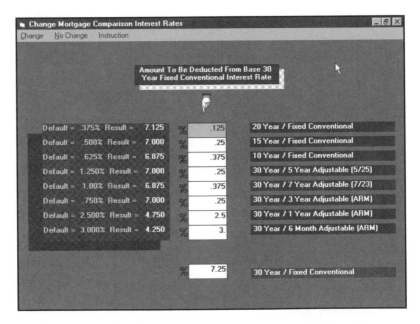

First, go the Estimate module (the Main Screen) and enter a rate for the 30-year fixed-rate conventional loan. Set your "mortgage type" for "30 YR Fixed/Conventional." Then, go to the Values screen. This will establish the figure you entered as the baseline setting for rate comparisons.

Use Web sites such as HSH Associates (www.hsh.com), and www.maze.com to get current interest rates for different types of loans. Another source of rate information is the financial section of the newspaper.

With only the basics about your financial profile, that is, your monthly gross income and monthly obligation and how much cash you have for a down payment, you can do a quick calculation of your capacity.

Compare this to your income requirements and monthly payment associated with a 20-year fixed, 15-year fixed, 10-year fixed, and a combination of fixed and adjustable-rate products by changing the mortgage type and adjusting the interest rate.

Notice the higher income requirements for the low-rate 15-year and 10-year fixed conventional loans.

In the Maze Master's opinion . . .
If you do not qualify for a shorter-term, lower-interest
rate mortgage now, perhaps that will change soon.
What do you do? Refinance.

NEG AM ARM—THREE PAYMENT OPTIONS

If you are a medium- to high-risk borrower who has a keen sense of cash flow grounded in good financial planning skills, then you may want the level of control that a *negatively amortizing* (neg am) ARM will give you. This loan has an unjustifiably bad reputation.

In the Maze Master's opinion . . .
A negatively amortizing loan (neg am) is the "extreme
control ARM," or the "maximum option loan."

Look at what the neg am proposition means in terms of dollars and cents before you get overwhelmed by the financing jargon and popular notions of what it involves.

Neg ams include a teaser period of usually 1, 3, or 6 months, during which the payments are fully amortized at an attractive interest rate. Each period will have an annual payment cap of $7\frac{1}{2}$% (maximum) and a lifetime interest rate cap of approximately 6% over the start rate. The caps are fixed for the life of the loan. There are usually 3 different payment options:

1. The minimum payment, based on the start rate, with a payment cap of 7.5 percent per year. This minimum could move one of two ways: If the cap moves up to the maximum 7.5 percent, then the start-rate payment × 107.5 percent = second year's minimum monthly payment. If the cap moves down the maximum 7.5 percent, then the start-rate payment × 92.5 percent = second year's minimum monthly payment. It is highly unlikely in the first 3 years that your payments will take a dive. In fact, count on them going up.

   With this option, you keep the lender happy by paying a required minimum interest, but unless you make some kind of principal payment occasionally, your principal balance will actually increase.

2. A fully-indexed, interest-only payment. With this option, you pay an amount that keeps your principal balance the same, unless you make an occasional principal payment.

3. A fully amortized payment, which equals the then-current balance × the then-current remaining amortized period, fully indexed interest rate × the remaining amortization period.

   With this option, you have a standard situation in which you pay principal plus interest.

The minimum payment for a loan can be surprisingly low. For the first month, it would consist of a base interest rate—the teaser rate—plus an amount to reduce the principal. After the first month, or teaser period that extends more than one month, it would be a below-interest-only-payment based on your start rate. The payment is not enough to reduce principal and is normally below the amount of an interest-only payment.

On a randomly selected day, the interest rate for such a loan was 2.95 percent, and the COFI (Cost of Funds Index) was 5.116 percent with a margin of 2.5 percent.

Here is how the 3 payment options would look at the outset for a $100,000 loan:

Option #1. Introductory interest rate + principal payment = initial payment. That means 2.95 percent interest + principal = $418.91 during the teaser period.

This first monthly payment, or payments, during the teaser period is the last time that the minimum payment reduces principal in addition to paying interest due. It includes an astonishing $173 in principal reduction, which affects the balance on which any future interest is calculated. After the teaser period, however, the minimum payment is strictly a less-than-interest-only payment with no amount going toward principal reduction; the difference between Options #1 and #2 is the amount of negative amortization. Using Option #1 will keep your lender satisfied because you are paying interest on your balance, but it isn't enough to either reduce the principal or keep up with the then-current interest rate.

On the pro side, using Option #1 in a given month eases any cash flow problems you have. It enables you to make a timely mortgage payment in cash-poor month. On the con side, you actually add to the principal balance if you do not make a payment to reduce principal by the end of the calendar year. If you use select Option #1 all the time without earmarking funds for principal reduction, you'll find yourself with a higher principal balance than when you got the loan! Instead of having the neg am loan work to your financial advantage, you will find that it leads to, or compounds, financial trouble.

Option #2. Index + margin = fully indexed rate. That means 5.116 percent + 2.5 percent = 7.62 percent for an interest-only payment of $633.90.

The important note here is a reminder that this payment is interest-only. Option #2 enables you to keep the lender satisfied, but it neither reduces principal nor adds to your principal balance.

This payment is ideal because it gives you a flat position. You have the ability to maintain your loan balance without any increase in principal. It gives you the maximum tax advantage with the least amount of payment in conjunction with one of the most stable indices available.

Then, if you feel compelled to make a principal payment—$25, $150, $1,000—you can do it at your own speed, with the reduction in principal more closely felt than in almost any other situation. This is because the program adjusts payments yearly, but the interest formula allows for a reduction in principal to be savored in the next 30-day payment.

Option #3. Fully indexed rate × remaining balance, amortized over the remaining period. At 7.62 percent interest, payment = $706.74 = 30-year fully amortized payment.

This is the "plain vanilla" ARM payment formula, equivalent to the payment you would make on an ARM that doesn't move for the remaining period (an unrealistic concept). Think of Option #3 as a Polaroid instant photo for a 30-day period: With a 30-year ARM, that monthly adjustment would have to be like 360 identical snapshots.

A more dramatic example of the difference in ARM payment options is a negatively amortizing loan of $500,000 for a 40-year period, which is quite reasonable. Using the same rates as those that applied to the above loan, your numbers would look like this.

Option #1 monthly payment:	$1,775.54
Option #2 monthly payment:	$3,173.00
Option #3 monthly payment:	$3,333.30

In this case, $1,397.46—the difference between payment Option #1 and Option #2—would be added to the principal balance if you paid Option #1. If you paid Option #2, your maximum interest payment is made without a principal payment, but you are not adding to your principal balance. Then again, every time you make a payment earmarked to reduce your principal balance, you also reduce the interest owed on that balance. In a short-term, practical sense, that means you have reduced the interest on the next payment.

In the Maze Master's opinion . . .
If you are a Christmas-tree or pumpkin-farm vendor,
or a partner in a firm that allows generous holiday bonuses,
consider getting a neg am loan.

The negatively amortizing loan is a great tool for someone who regularly receives a large cash influx at a particular time of the year. Options #1 and #2 allow you to stay current with payments while you plan for an infusion of capital allowing you to dramatically reduce your principal.

The negatively amortizing option is a winning scenario in terms of income taxes, too. If you allow the loan to go neg am for the first 11 months of the calendar year, you have not only increased your loan balance, but you have paid (tax-deductible) interest on (tax-deductible) interest. In the 12th month, if you make a payment that brings your principal balance down to where it sat on January 1 of that year, you can have a sizable deduction without realizing any increase in your loan balance. The advantage, of course, depends on how you do your accounting and whether or not the IRS makes any changes in the tax-deductibility of mortgage-related interest. In the section on Matching Loan Type to Collateral, you will see how this approach can still lead to a build in equity.

Even if you make a less-than interest-only payment (Option #1), the neg am can be a wise decision if your property is appreciating more than the amount of negative amortization.

In terms of your timeline, you should think about everything that impacts your finances day-to-day, month-to-month, and year-to-year, if you want to determine what the most ideal loan package is for you.

THE SECOND STEP TO LOAN SELECTION: PERSONAL OPPORTUNITY

Having made choices about which loan suits you, your next challenge is to determine what a lender thinks will suit you. At which rate will the lender qualify you for which loan product? Based on your capacity, credit, and collateral, lenders will automatically make judgments about which loan you should seek.

The lender's artificial intelligence may indicate, for example, that you don't qualify for a $240,000 loan on a 30-year fixed, but do qualify on a 5-year fixed that rolls into an ARM. What are the capacity, credit and collateral factors that make a difference?

Matching Loan Type to Capacity and Credit

Up to this point, loan products have been categorized in terms of repayment options, but can also be discussed in terms of limits on the loan amount: conventional, VA, FHA, Fannie Mae, or Freddie Mac. You should consult a broker or lending agent if you think your limits on capacity and other special conditions enable you to qualify for government-insured programs. Your decisions regarding these types will depend on your capacity (your ability to handle debt) and your credit worthiness (borrowing power).

Conventional. As the name implies, a *conventional* mortgage is a standard loan. It is not obtained under a government-insured program, such as a Veterans Administration (VA) or Federal Housing Administration (FHA) loan.

VA. Applicable only to veterans of United States military service, the VA loan has a current limit of around $200,000, but that amount is increased periodically. Lenders will often relax the rules on credit to help veterans qualify.

FHA. The FHA is a federal agency that insures first mortgage. It enables lenders to loan a very high percentage of the sale price.

Fannie Mae and Freddie Mac. Although their guidelines reflect similar restrictions on loan amounts, these quasi-governmental agencies do have some differences in what they allow. For example, Freddie Mac will allow ratios of the borrower and co-borrower to be combined, even if the co-borrower(s) has no plan to occupy the property. Fannie Mae does not allow a non-occupant's ratios to be co-mingled with the primary borrower's.

Conforming vs Jumbo Loans. Another method of typing loans is by the amount of money required: a *conforming* loan and a *jumbo* loan. Basically, a conforming loan is under $207,000, and a jumbo is more than that. But you might find that number changing because of economic shifts upward and downward. There may also be some geographic variation, especially in Hawaii and Alaska, where the limit on a conforming loan is higher than in the continental United States.

Matching Loan Type to Collateral

Certain types of collateral do not enhance your chances of getting a mortgage or getting concessions on a loan product from a lender. Key considerations are price, condition and location of the subject property. Problems can arise when the property is overpriced in relation to its condition and/or location; the condition of the collateral makes it less marketable than comparable properties in the same neighborhood, or makes it hard to insure; or the location makes it less marketable than comparable properties elsewhere, or makes it hard to insure.

Outside of New York City, for example, you could face anything from refusal to extraordinary caveats if you try to finance a condominium above the 7th floor of a building because the hook and ladder won't go above 7 stories.

Certain characteristics of a property that give it *functional obsolescence* also raise concerns for a lender. Examples would include a house with one bathroom, but four bedrooms in a family neighborhood where comparable properties have two bathrooms or a house with no garage or carport in a neighborhood where parking is difficult and other properties have private parking associated with them.

Collateral can provide some planned, and unplanned, advantages in relation to a mortgage, too. In December 1995, heavy rains in San Francisco caused the collapse of an old sewer system. This created a sinkhole that swallowed a house valued at about $1.3 million. Real estate agents joked that property across the street, which had an obstructed view of the Golden Gate Bridge and the San Francisco Bay prior to the accident and a market value of roughly $800,000, immediately jumped in value by half a million dollars.

What if the owners of the house across the street had a neg am loan? If they had paid the minimum amount, or Option #1, to boost their tax deductions, and brought their balance back to the starting amount at the end of each year, they would suddenly have acquired a huge amount of *equity* without ever having lowered their principal balance! Just because their house escalated in value, and their original loan was based on a much lower value, their equity position would have become very strong.

Consider how your equity position could be dramatically affected by a fortuitous change in the value of your property. Let's say your original down payment on a $1 million loan was 20 percent; your LTV was 80 percent. You paid Option #1 on your neg am loan and let your principal balance build up to $900,000, or a 90 percent

LTV. The house across the street falls off a cliff, giving you a beautiful view of the water and boats in the harbor. The value of your house escalates to $1.6 million. Your LTV is now down to 60 percent.

In the Maze Master's opinion . . .
Buy the worst house in the nicest neighborhood.

This is a phenomenon you can plan for if you follow this advice, and pair it with a loan that frees up enough cash to improve your property:

Using the extra cash you may have by paying Option #1 or Option #2 to finance property improvements can build your equity position without your having to reduce your principal balance one dime. You give yourself enormous financial leverage when you match your loan product to your collateral and your plans for it.

The following story of a property conveys an extreme case of the importance of collateral. Although the subject property was rental, the message is clear: What you own, plan to own, or have rights to, can have a powerful impact on your financial leverage.

TRUE STORY: AIR RIGHTS HELP LEASE VALUE SOAR

The owner of a restaurant in a one-story building in the financial district of San Francisco had a 50-year lease on the space. Halfway into the lease, a very large bank bought the block, and had plans to develop every inch of it. The restaurateur was successful and wanted to stay.

Given that the restaurateur had inalienable long-term rights to the space, the large financial institution decided to build around it. The company planned to surround and literally cover the relatively tiny structure. The plan couldn't be realized, however, because the leaseholder had claimed *air rights*, stating that a property owner owns everything upward. Generally speaking, air rights contain an easement to accommodate flying aircraft, and rarely does anyone worry about anything beyond that.

With the restaurant owner's claim airtight, the large financial institution had no choice. Architectural plans to overtake the building either had to be scrapped, or the restaurant owners had to be convinced financially that the plan was in their best interests.

The owner of the little restaurant, whose long-term lease enabled him to pay very low rent in relation to comparable properties, held fast. The large financial institution was forced to buy them out. The bank bought the restaurant owner's air rights at a price reportedly over $20 million.

A Guide to Selecting Your Loan

The chart on the next page condenses some of the characteristics which could describe the borrower and the loan and help you make the right mortgage choice.

BORROWER	LOAN	
Fixed Rate Mortgages:		
Very low risk tolerance Long timeline (i.e., plan to stay a while) Stable capacity, with no major shifts anticipated Planning to retire in 30 years	30 year/fixed	• Fewest variables • Most difficult to qualify for
Same as above, but capacity stronger	20, 15, or 10 year/fixed	• Shorter term • Higher payment • Tougher to get
ARMS:		
Medium risk tolerance Good planning associated with capacity Long timeline	ARM	• Qualify for more money than a fixed
Medium risk tolerance (increases to high if planning ability poor) Good planning associated with capacity And/or capacity involves large cash influx at a particular time of year and/or plans to dramatically improve collateral	Negative Amortizing ARM payment options: 1. Less than interest only (negative amortization) 2. interest only 3. fully amortized, with possibility of 40-year term	• Best potential tax benefits
FIRMS:		
Medium risk tolerance Plans to move in 3, 5, or 7 years; plans to improve collateral; or in high-income years, has ability to pay off but needs a tax break, (i.e., something will change in 3, 5, or 7 years)	30 year/3, 5, or 7 year adjustable	• Timeline is key issue • Low rate (low risk) for fixed period of time
Balloons:		
High risk tolerance Great planning associated with capacity And/or large cash reserve	Balloon	• Definite maturity date • Lower rate than FIRM at the same point

Chapter 6

Pit Stop: Packaging
Your Parts for the Lender

Packaging yourself correctly for a lender can be the difference between approval and rejection. It is a matter of matching the right documentation with underwriting requirements. You want to give the lender what is needed according to the rules to approve funding for a particular loan product. There are several types of underwriting packages, one of which helps you discover which package would present you in the best light, rather than causing the lights to go out. Sometimes more is not necessarily better and often a combination of skill and finesse create a successful package.

Finally, accurate completion of the loan application known as Fannie Mae Form 1003, and Freddie Mac Form 65 becomes very important to navigating the Mortgage Maze.

UNDERWRITING GUIDELINES: WHO MAKES UP THIS STUFF?

In Chapter 1, you got a sense of how the secondary market is a powerful influence on underwriting guidelines. To protect the investor in the lending institution, requirements have gone from suggestions to guidelines to rules. Now let's consider specifically who makes the rules.

While Fannie Mae and Freddie Mac play a significant role in shaping underwriting rules, individual lending institutions can create their own, sometimes without much regard for the guideline templates of the quasi-governmental agencies.

The short answer to the question, "Who makes the rules?" is the Golden Rule: "Whoever has the gold makes the rules." The more powerful the lending institution is in terms of assets, the greater its ability to originate loans. The greater the volume of loans, the stronger its ability to play in the secondary mortgage market and the more capacity it has to create its own set of underwriting guidelines. The many variances between guidelines can make shopping lender to lender drive you mad with paperwork.

The following illustration shows that the mortgage lending cycle begins and ends with you as the depositor/investor in a financial system that also loans you money.

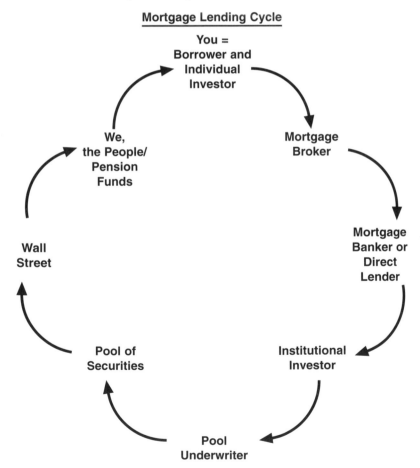

Mortgage Lending Cycle

In the lending process you are both the borrower and the investor in securities that would not be stable without a sound system of underwriting. To phrase it simply, the underwriting guidelines protect you from yourself.

You begin the process by going to a mortgage broker or loan officer at a lending institution to secure a loan. The broker or loan officer packages you (complete with gift wrap and bows) for the mortgage banker, who is a conduit of funds from a lender or may be the lending institution itself. The lender has plans to sell loans to Wall Street investment firms ("the street") or to the secondary market. Therefore the loan must be *securitized*, or insured. The stricter the underwriting rules the more securitized is the loan. The impact on you is that everyone along the chain requires more and perhaps different documentation of your capacity, credit, and collateral. It's like everyone looking at the same picture through different lenses. Anytime your numbers fall short of their particular standard marks, compensating factors which may relate to your character must surface. By the time your package has made it a third of the way through the chain, you have gone through several rounds of scrutiny by different humans and different computers.

The next step relates to how your loan is sold. Related loan products are grouped in *pools* and sold by the lender. A pool would probably have a mix of property types—single-family homes, duplexes to fourplexes, owner- and non-owner-occupied dwellings—but it would contain mortgages with the same terms so the pool moves synchronously. Characteristics of a pool of 30-year fixed loans, for example, would include similar interest rates and remaining life of the mortgages. In technical terms the pool would be described by its *weighted average coupon* (WAC), the average interest rate, and *weighted average maturity* (WAM), the number of months remaining on a 360-month loan. There are other loan elements that would not be consistent for members of the pool, however, such as the same life cap on rates, or identical margins. An investor might compose an 11th District Cost-of-Funds ARM pool worth $500 million, and sell it back to a large savings and loan institution. If that same S&L contributed loans to that pool, in buying back the same loan, it has turned liabilities into assets on its balance sheet!

Before the loan can join a pool, the institutional investor is required to have a mortgage insurance company or pool underwriter. The *pool underwriter* is a third party with no relationship to the pool or investment. He or she certifies that ample evidence exists that the loan contains all the characteristics that make it worthy of pool insurance and is securitizable. Statistically, investors know that a certain percentage of the loans will go into default, only because there is no way to underwrite for major illness, death, divorce, and other unexpected interruptions in the borrower's financial life. Nevertheless, the securitization process involving the pool underwriter reduces the possibility that anything other than a disaster will cause a default.

Once your loan package gets a stamp of approval from the professional underwriting company, or whatever entity served as the pool underwriter, you will most likely get your loan. As part of a pool, your loan then goes into a security. This transaction is transparent to you the borrower except when it causes a delay in your processing. You don't know what happened to your loan because as long as the company that controls the duties of a mortgagee and *services your loan* remains the same, you send your payments to the same entity.

Prior to the mid-1980s, when the shift toward stricter underwriting guidelines occurred, a loan was not submitted for pool approval until after the lender approved it. Under this system, the percentage of loans that earned pool approval was so low, the lender had to guarantee the loan for a period of up to two years, or guarantee the first 10 percent of losses. Needless to say, reserve requirements for lenders were high, so they welcomed the reversal of steps. Naturally, it added to the processing time and qualifying factors for the consumer.

Next Wall Street or the secondary mortgage market invests in the securities. Finally, individuals, pension funds, money managers handling corporate investment, and institutions themselves invest in the mortgage-backed securities.

Essentially, everybody is satisfying everybody else back to the person who has a $2,000 IRA in a mortgage-backed security. If you are a borrower who owns mortgage-backed instruments in your pension fund or through any other investment means, in a way you are your own lender. The system has protected your investments by making it tough for you to borrow.

THE ART AND SCIENCE OF PACKAGING FOR UNDERWRITERS

In the world of competitive racing, drivers pull into the pit to have the car checked, fueled, and fixed by ace mechanics. A pit stop gets the machine in shape for victory, or it might be blamed for causing defeat. Whether you win or lose, you still have to make the stop.

You are now at a pit stop in the Mortgage Maze. You have a good idea, if not a firm one, of which loan product you are heading toward. You also have some ability to gauge the opportunities ahead. All you need to do now is compose a package for the underwriter that makes it possible, and easy, to close the deal. In homebuying, you want to settle for nothing less than victory! And in refinancing, you want to settle for nothing less than lower payments, and to be in a position to quickly recoup your costs.

Not too long ago, packaging yourself was a function of the Old-Boys' Club, a network of buddies and acquaintances. Prior to the current standard of securitization, a banker would instruct one of his loan officers to put a package together for a friend or preferred customer, then he would fund the loan. This lack of oversight contributed to the notorious savings and loan crisis of the late 1980s.

People who remember "the good old days" think they can still carve out a deal instantly because they have $50,000 in a bank account where they know the banker. This is no longer sufficient clout, and you can be grateful for that. As much as securitization makes you endure paperwork nightmares, it is a great equalizer and an important balancing force in the economy.

TRUE STORY: BIG MONEY, NO SPECIAL DEAL

Carmine Longwood had a monumental cash flow by most people's standards. Each month, he pushed $300,000 to $400,000 through his accounts, although he could put his hands on only $100,000 at any one time. Carmine assumed that because he kept a portfolio worth $6 million at one securities firm and another one handled hundreds of thousands of dollars a month in day trading for him, he would qualify for a special deal, or *portfolio loan*, with one of them.

He went to the securities firm that held the $6 million investment portfolio and applied for a $1.2 million loan for a property with a *fair market value* of $1.6 million. He was rejected because he could not substantiate sufficient income or cash reserves to qualify under the underwriting guidelines.

The Securities and Exchange Commission (SEC), an agency of the federal government, has oversight over securities companies, and they are even stricter in enforcing securities guidelines than other types of lenders.

The choices you face in packaging for the underwriter all relate to which paper you want to use and how much of it you need. The central packaging issues relate to the best way to present your capacity and credit and what should or should not be said about your collateral and character. In many instances, you will have to determine whether standard documentation, like a *verification of rent* (VOR), or the equally acceptable alternative documentation of 12 months of canceled checks will present you most favorably while satisfying the lender's need-to-know. If your landlord dislikes you, or you want to avoid disclosing your plan to move out until you get final approval on a loan, submit the 12 months of canceled checks.

Based on their delay in cashing rent checks, some landlords don't seem to care when their tenants pay. If your landlord routinely waits to deposit your rent checks, you will have a problem proving that you paid on time. At that point, you have to request a VOR or letter of recommendation from your landlord unless you had the foresight to use certified mail or another special postal or courier service to deliver the check.

Your four basic choices of underwriting packages, in order of volume of documentation from least to most, are 1) *no income*; 2) *quick qualifier*; 3) *limited*, or *alternative documentation*; and 4) *full documentation*. As you will soon see, the names for these packages can be very misleading.

No Income Package

"No income loan" implies what you don't tell the lender, not what you don't earn! A no income stated package means that you build a case for your capacity without telling the lender how much you make. You must leave the income section of the application blank and provide no tax returns or pay stubs. Through other documents, the lender gets a sense of your monthly income, and qualifies you on the basis of assets, credit and collateral.

A vital element in this package is evidence of your cash position: either the *verification of deposit* (*VOD*) for your bank accounts or bank statements. If you provide bank statements, the lender will attempt to figure out your income based on money deposited on a monthly basis. The lender will also cross-reference your statements to ensure that no income is counted twice and review them to determine if you transferred funds from one account to another. Duplication will be subtracted from your income. The irony, as you can see, is that the lender will do everything possible to determine your income on a no-income loan.

 A verification of deposit gives the lender information on your current balance and averages over the last 60 to 90 days. Provide the VOD rather than bank statements, since the least amount of information invites the least number of questions and scrutiny. Make the lender request statements if it can be demonstrated that they are necessary—and question the reason for the request unless it is clear to you that the lender is being reasonable.

The lender will also want documentation on 12 months of debt service for all obligations stated on your application that is not on your credit report.

> ### In the Maze Master's opinion . . .
> You should not tell your life story in your loan application.

Use your credit report as your base document for listing debt on your application. The credit report is what the lender sees, so the loan application should reflect what it says. With the no income package some lenders also want between 80 to 100 percent of your yearly income in the bank as reserves. In addition, your credit has to be perfect and your collateral sound. It is not uncommon for a lender to order two appraisals on a no income stated loan. Facing requirements like this, you will agree the lender's motto is "Prove to me you don't need the money, and I'll give you a loan." To maintain your perspective on the situation, remember that the lender's agenda is dominated by risk avoidance.

For the borrower who has assets and cash influx, without the standard employment situation, a no-income stated loan package highlights your ability to pay without distracting the loan officer with the non-standard features of your financial profile. In the majority of cases, this package is only available to self-employed borrowers. Occasionally, a lender will allow a salaried spouse, as a non-head-of-household, to be included. The spouse simply states occupation and place of employment.

Normally, the lender will confirm that you are self-employed and have a place of business by phoning directory assistance and asking for a listing; the lender may also call to see if the phone is answered like a business phone. In addition, expect to be asked for a business license. The lender will corroborate your spouse's claim by calling the personnel department of the employer listed on the application.

You will find yourself sailing off the cliff if you attempt a no income package and don't have the required business license. Find out what the regulation is in your jurisdiction, and get the license. The fee is usually minimal, and compliance is well worth it.

The no income package usually supports loans with an LTV that is no higher than 75 percent, a deal in which you make at least a 25 percent down payment.

To summarize the essential components of the no income stated underwriting package, you need the following:

1. VOD and/or bank statements, which document down payment, reserves, and deposits.

2. Credit report, bank statements or canceled checks to document debt service.

3. A credit report reflecting an excellent record of payment.

4. A minimum of 25 percent down payment.

5. Cash-reserve requirements vary, but can be as high as 80 to 100 percent of your gross annual income, and as little as 2 to 3 months PITI.

6. Sound collateral; the lender will go through the contract and require any reports that you requested in addition to the appraisal, as well as any reports the appraiser has requested because of problems spotted.

A verification of deposit revealing a lack of *seasoned funds*, a level of funds that has been in your account less than 60 to 90 days, will raise the lender's eyebrows. If your current balance listed on the VOD differs significantly from the average balance, a lender will suspect that you borrowed money in an attempt to give your financial profile a facelift.

The credit report will also show any debt and payment schedule in conflict with amounts listed on the application and could also reflect liens for spousal and child support. If these items surface, you will need a sound explanation or will have to change course.

A study of the no income package, which is the most streamlined of all methods, reveals a core truth about how underwriters look at your financial credentials. Some aspects are clearly in focus, while others contribute to the background. In the case of the no income package, the underwriter focuses on the down payment and LTV first, cash reserves second, and finally cash flow and other compensating factors.

QUICK QUALIFIER PACKAGE

"Quick qualifier" is an oxymoron. This loan package may make your process quicker than with a full documentation loan, because you have less exposure, but it isn't quick in an absolute sense.

Recall that the lender loans to those who don't need the money. With a quick qualifier (QQ), the premise is that you can lessen your load by proving that you don't need the money.

Like the no income package, the quick qualifier normally requires no verification of income. Here again, you will need alternative documentation of your assets and payment history. However, your top and bottom ratios have to be right and your credit, perfect.

Like the no income package, the quick qualifier is often associated with the self-employed borrower. It is also appropriate for borrowers with significant investments whose income is from dividends and interest. As long as assets and investments can be verified, the lender will nod approvingly.

TRUE STORY: FULL DOC OR BUST

Susan Melon insisted that she wanted a "full doc" or full documentation loan so she would get the lowest possible rate. She had $348,000 in the bank, and wanted to buy a $279,000 property, putting 20 percent down. In school full-time, Susan's tax returns showed she has $30,000 in annual adjusted gross income, all from rental properties, interest and dividends. Unfortunately, she needed $72,000 income to qualify under the guidelines. With $250,000 in a stock portfolio, and $98,000 in cash, she cried, "I can't believe I can't do a full doc loan!" when her broker advised her to do a quick qualifier. The reality is this. With good credit and plenty of assets, but an insufficient income stream, Susan is a perfect candidate for a no-income loan or, possibly, a quick qualifier if she promotes herself as a self-employed investor.

Susan found a different broker who developed the full doc loan. When her package was submitted to Freddie Mac and rejected, she closed a number of doors. Freddie Mac keeps good records, and she won't be able to go back with a different package. She ended up with a loan that was oппоnsive, in terms of points paid at closing, and faced refinancing within the next 12 to 18 months.

The primary difference between a quick qualifier package and a no-income stated package is that you will need to submit an IRS form 4506 allowing the lender to secure your tax returns. The no income package verifies bank deposits, VOD and/or bank statements to document reserves and to back into income through the amounts deposited.

However, both the no income and the quick qualifier packages require bank statements or canceled checks to document debt service not reported on the credit report, a credit report reflecting an excellent record of payment, a minimum of 20 percent down payment, cash reserves equaling 20 to 50 percent of your stated gross annual income, or three to six months of PITI, depending on the lender, and sound collateral, verified by a standard appraisal.

Some lenders will not accept a self-employed borrower with more than 25 percent of his/her annual income from passive sources, such as investments.

Loans like the no income and QQ are priced with *premiums*, so the lender is earning more. In some cases, the lender may not assess the risk position as thoroughly as possible. To make things even more complicated, all lenders' focus is not the same. Much to their ultimate dismay, many borrowers may be less diligent on a QQ loan because they realize that lenders need to make profitable loans and hope to avoid intense scrutiny by paying the premium

If you do manage to contort or distort your income to make it appear larger, you could be in for an unpleasant surprise. When they are the least bit suspicious of your documentation, lenders will use the clout of an IRS 4506 (see Appendix C) to satisfy their need for undisputed evidence of your income. If the 4506 reveals a 15 percent or more variation, the lender may revoke the loan approval, request additional documentation, or make a counter offer under another loan program.

The latest IRS form is a 9501, which allows the IRS to verify quickly what the adjusted gross income (AGI) of the borrower is. Again, if there is a discrepancy between what you report and what the IRS reports, get out your explaining stationery.

TRUE STORY: TRUTH OR DARE

Henry Wormwood, an import-export dealer who spent long periods of time out of the country, came to a broker with his request to do a quick qualifier. He had $85,000 in the bank and wanted to buy a $275,000 property. His credit record was spotty as a dalmation, so the broker told him that no-income stated and QQ were out of the question. The broker recommended that Henry go with a full docs loan priced with a premium because of his poor credit record. Then he could refinance in 12 to 24 months after reestablishing a good payment history. Henry disregarded the advice.

Another broker packaged Henry as a QQ and went to a lender who responded with a favorable response dependent on a counter offer: The lender wanted to see two years of W2s (the forms filed with a tax return) that document employment income. This changed the nature of the loan package, but the product still seemed desirable enough to the broker that he urged Henry to comply. Henry dutifully supplied his broker with two years of W2s that stated the amount of income he needed to qualify for the loan.

Generally satisfied with the documentation, the lender funded the loan, but also used form 4506 to order Henry's tax returns from the IRS. When they arrived six weeks later after the loan funded, the tax returns revealed that Henry's W2s were custom-designed for the lender. They stated his income as more than double the amount on the returns. Henry alleged that he merely provided what his broker requested: W2s documenting a certain level of income. Finger pointing ensued, but it never distracted the lender from the fundamental truth: The QQ was based on a fraud.

At that point, Henry's life became a maze of legal and financial troubles. The lender demanded repayment of the loan if Henry wanted to avoid charges. And even with repay ment the lender was obliged to report a case of fraud against a public institution.

Henry's ultimate path was to borrow the money from a private source. Then, instead of having a 5/25 FIRM at a rate of 8 percent for the initial five-year period, he paid 13 per cent interest plus 6 points, a fee equivalent to 6 percent of the loan amount.

The borrower's attempt to save less than $1,000 in fees ended up costing him over 10 times that amount plus attor ney's fees and marked him as a fraud with the authorities.

LIMITED OR ALTERNATIVE DOCUMENTATION

The limited or alternative documentation (alt doc) package proves capacity through the normal sources. It is an accommodation to the borrower in that you have alternatives in the way you satisfy the underwriting requirements to secure the loan as fast as possible.

Rather than requesting verifications of deposit, employment and mortgage or rent, for example, you can quickly assemble the papers in your desk drawer that legitimately document your assets over the previous 90 days and your income history over the past 2 tax years and year-to-date. To show income and available cash, you can provide 3 months current bank statements instead of VOD.

 Bank statements can turn into a credit report if you give statements that reflect overdrafts.

To prove salary and demonstrate employment history, you can use 2 years of W2s, plus pay stubs covering the last 30 days that contain year-to-date income figures instead of verification of employment. If you are non-salaried and/or a 1099 employee, supply 2 years of tax returns and a year-to-date profit-and-loss (P&L) statement if you apply beyond 90 days into a new calendar year.

To demonstrate timely payment of mortgage or rent, furnish 12 months of canceled checks instead of verification of mortgage or verification of rent forms. To verify other assets and their value, provide statements of your trust account, pension fund, whole life insurance statements, or other investments. You need to present two statements that show a beginning and an end balance for the most recent 2- to 3-month period. Or in the case of stocks or bonds that you hold in certificate form, you can include a copy of stock and bond certificates and a copy of the day's newspaper listing or other evidence of current worth.

In the Maze Master's opinion . . .
In a limited doc loan package, you probably won't need copies of your stock certificates if you've already verified 30 to 50 percent of your annual salary with bank statements.

Add to these items a good credit report, and you have the ability to walk into a lender and get approval immediately. Okay, so that's a slight exaggeration. Even with a credit history that is flawed in the distant past, but good for the most recent 24 months and reflects no mortgage lates and past-due items, explanatory letters could still get your package processed quickly.

In supplying canceled checks, be sure both sides of the check have been copied. Don't even think about trying to match the back side of one check with the front side of another to convince a lender that you always paid your mortgage or rent on time. Checks are encoded on both sides and it is easy for a lender to spot a mismatch.

In the Maze Master's opinion . . .
If you were late paying a bill, or even several bills, and had a good reason, a letter of explanation will serve you far better than deceit.

FULL DOCUMENTATION PACKAGE

A full docs loan is an invitation to the lender to examine the intimate details of your financial life. There are no secrets, no attempt to conceal the dents, scratches, or clunking noises. Clearly, arming the lender with so much positive information minimizes risk for the lending institution. For that reason, when a lender decides to approve a full docs or alt docs loan, the terms of the offer are normally more desirable than with other underwriting packages. You may not have much money to put down—perhaps only 5 percent or less—but you are a known quantity, therefore, a measurable risk.

Following is a list of documents that would be found in a full docs loan package:

- Residential Loan Application

- Residential Mortgage Credit Report

- Supplements to Credit Reports (if applicable), such as letters from credit grantors

- Borrower's Credit Explanations (if applicable)

- Verification of mortgage/rent, *or* 12 months cancelled checks, *or* a letter from the owner of your rental property, *or* bank statements that verify mortgage/rent payment

- Business Credit Report for self-employed borrowers, normally if loan amount is over $600,000 or if you are the sole proprietor, but some lenders always require

- Current year-to-date pay stub and past 2 years' W2s *or* Verification of Employment

- Verification of previous employment, if less than 2 years at the current job

- Written explanation of employment/gap letter (if applicable)

- Written letter of intent to seek employment for working spouse that is relocating due to head of household relocation. This will allow the use of trailing spouse income, if necessary

- Self-employed borrowers should include the following:

- Current YTD P&L

- 2 years' Federal Tax Returns with all schedules and K1s

- 2 years' Partnership/Corporate Returns with all schedules if ownership in the corporation is 0 to 10 percent

- Copy of Business License

- Accountant's name, address and phone number for verification purposes

- Current lease for all rental properties

- Verification of assets (current 2 months' bank statements) *or* verification of deposits (VOD)

- Gift letter (if applicable)

- Verification of donor's availability of funds (if funds not received by borrower)

- Verification of transfer of gift funds (donor's withdrawal and borrower's deposit or donor's canceled check)

- Earnest money deposit verification, normally if over 2 percent of contract sales price

- Executed sales contract/HUD-1 on current residence (if applicable, for source of funds or release of liability if sold), or escrow information

- Divorce decree, separation agreement, or bifurcation agreement (if applicable)

- Executed sales contract/escrow instructions of subject property

- Standard FNMA/FHLMC Appraisal, including three photos

- Handwritten FNMA 1003 executed by all borrowers (Note: General Authorization Form is not required if handwritten FNMA 1003 is signed and dated by all borrowers)

- Disclosures: Initial Truth-in-Lending, Good Faith Estimate, and any other applicable state and federal law disclosures

- Preliminary title report

 If you elect to use the services of a mortgage broker, that professional will do a better job for you if you come in with as much documentation as possible. It is easier to shape 10 pounds of clay into a perfect 2-pound vase than it is to start with a 1-pound lump and add to it.

At this stage, ask yourself, "Why complete a two-ton, full documentation loan exposing every inch of myself under a bright light when I might be able to get away with a couple scraps of paper about my assets and credit?" The reason is that everything in underwriting is on a risk-reward basis. A lender who has the ability to make concessions because of how loans are priced at that institution will do it for a price if certain conditions are met. That is, you must present "compensating factors." So, if you go to the lender with something less than a full doc or alt doc loan, but your loan fits well into the institution's portfolio, and it came from a solid originating source such as a known broker, and/or you had strong compensating factors like perfect credit, the lender may make a concession and approve the loan. Everytime a concession is made on documentation, ratios, and so on, your rates and/or fees will go up. The reason that a borrower can benefit with a full doc loan, then, is because the rates will almost always be lower than with any of the other packages.

PUTTING THE (RIGHT) FACTS IN THE APPLICATION

The preface to Fannie Mae Form 1003, the residential loan application, contains critical instructions that many people pass over on their way to the blank boxes.

Those who rush straight to Part 1, only to exclaim, "How do they expect me to know this?" have ignored the first sentence: "This application is designed to be completed by the applicant(s) with the lender's assistance." It should be followed with the phrase "after you know what the market has to offer you." Attempting to complete the form before you know what you want can result in confusion for you and the lender.

The next sentence can cause turmoil if you are trying to borrow money with anyone except your spouse: "Applicants should complete this form as 'Borrower' or 'Co-Borrower,' as applicable." Unless your co-borrower is your spouse, in accordance with the laws of the land, your co-borrower must complete a separate application. This applies to mother-son combinations, or aunt-niece, or any other combination of blood relatives, as well as it applies to companions who are "together for life," yet not married.

The third sentence warns you of potential pitfalls (it's also exhausting in its length):

> Co-borrower information must also be provided (and the appropriate box checked) when the income or assets of a person other than the "Borrower" (including the Borrower's spouse) will be used as a basis for loan qualification or the income or assets of the Borrower's spouse will not be used as a basis for loan application, but his or her liabilities must be considered because the Borrower resides in a community property state, the security property is located in a community property state, or the Borrower is relying on other property located in a community property state as a basis for repayment of the loan.

If you live in a community property state and are married to someone with bad credit and/or a spouse you do not want involved in your property, the implications of this statement could be enormous. To financially disconnect yourself from your spouse, you should seek legal counsel and ensure that the proper paperwork is in place before you proceed with your loan application. There is no moral judgment implied in this. Many good couples avoid co-mingling funds because they have a keen understanding of their financial situation. This may include an obligation to maintain separate assets that will go to their heirs from a prior marriage, for example.

PART I

You can experiment with filling out the loan application from beginning to end by using a combination of QualifyR and the www.maze.com Web site.

The software calculators help you determine the income, asset, and debt figures that must be entered. The Web site form contains help every step of the way in filling out the block. The tips in this book expand the help provided at the site.

The following images are taken from www.maze.com.

I. TYPE OF MORTGAGE AND TERMS OF LOAN

Mortgage Applied for: `VA`   Amount: $ `[          ]`   Interest Rate: `2` `1/8`

No. Months: `180`   Amortization Type: `Fixed`

Part I of the Fannie Mae 1003 requests information that cannot be intelligently rendered until you know how your strengths and weaknesses fit with the loan products and conditions currently available.

PART II

Part II can only be addressed if you have selected a property. In that case, unless you are certain of the year in which the house was built, leave that space blank; fill in the address. You can respond to the request for a legal description of property with "see preliminary title report," you can leave the box blank, or you could fill in a precise description if you are certain of it.

There is often a fine line between a condominium (condo) and planned development (PUD), both of which are common interest developments (CIDs). The fundamental differences relate to ownership of *versus* rights to common areas, air rights, and ownership of land.

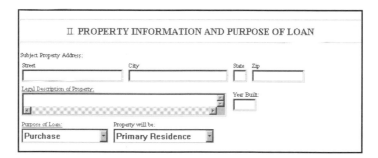

   The number of units really means, "How many separate homes are in this property?" A duplex would have two, for example. If the "property will be" statement is completed with either "primary residence" or "secondary residence," rather than "investment," the purpose of your loan is probably to purchase a home, refinance property, buy land, or construct a home. The types of loans corresponding to those purposes are purchase money, refinancing, land purchase, and construction.

   The completion for "estate will be held in" is either "fee simple" or "leasehold." Let someone else fill it out; the response will most likely be "fee simple."

Special questions in the middle of Part II address your need for a construction loan or refinancing. In this section, the lender is actually trying to ascertain your current debt in relation to original purchase price to get a thumbnail view of your equity position. A copy of Form 1003 with these elements is included as an annotated version at the www.maze.com Website.

 Save receipts for 100 percent of the materials you have put into the property, so you have original documentation of the cost and the details of improvements.

"Title will be held in what Name(s)" seems so straightforward. Enter the name of the person or people who will own the house—right? Assume nothing in the Mortgage Maze. Every block on the loan application has another layer of meaning or can lead to a complication! The name(s) you insert on the form must be identical to the name(s) signed on each and every official loan document executed at closing. Depending on how many forms, explanatory letters, and memos you must attach to the core documents, you could easily have dozens, or even scores, of papers to sign. If your full name is Natasha Alexandra Hypotenuse Triangle, you may want to use middle initials on the 1003.

Title will be held in what Name(s):

Manner in which Title will be held:

Source of Down Payment, Settlement Charges and/or Subordinate Financing:

Estate will be held in: Fee Simple   show expiration date:

There are six common ways in which the title may be held. The following explanation is an overview that hints at some of the complications, as outlined by the California Land Title Company of Marin (County).

Sole Ownership. 1. A Single Man/Woman means a man or woman who is not legally married.

2. An Unmarried Man/Woman means a man or woman, who having been married, is legally divorced.

3. A Married Man/Woman, as His/Her Sole and Separate Property means when a married individual wishes to acquire title in his or her name alone. The spouse must consent, by *quitclaim deed* or otherwise, to transfer thereby relinquishing all right, title, and interest in the property. If you are in a community property state, you have to look closely at how to hold title to property in this manner.

Co-Ownership. 4. Community Property is considered in a community property state. Property acquired by the husband and wife, jointly or separately, during their marriage is considered theirs together, unless there is a legal document that states otherwise. If one spouse dies without a will, the property most likely goes to the surviving spouse. If a spouse dies with a will, and leaves his or her half of the property to charity, a son or anyone else, that is the person's prerogative.

5. Joint Tenancy involves ownership of equal shares with the right of survivorship. When a joint tenant dies, title to the property immediately vests in the survivor or surviving joint tenants. Therefore, a joint tenant cannot dispose of the property in a will.

6. Tenancy in Common means that co-owners who are tenants in common own undivided interest, but they don't have to be equal in quantity or duration, as with joint tenancy. They may also arise at different times, and there is no right of survivorship. The share of a tenant in common goes to whomever the person designated in a will, or to next of kin.

The final question, addressing the source of your down payment and settlement charges, may also be one you will wish to answer later. As you enter into negotiations for a property or move toward closing, you might find that savings must be supplemented with liquidation of assets or a gift. Postpone filling this in until you have a firm grasp of your cash needs.

Parts III and IV

```
┌─────────────────────────────────────────────────────────────────────┐
│                      III.Borrower Information                         │
│  ─────────────────────────────────────────────────────────────────  │
│  Borrower's Name:                    Co-Borrower's Name:              │
│  [                        ]          [                        ]       │
│  Social Security Number:  Home Phone:  Social Security Number:  Home Phone: │
│  [          ]  [              ]      [          ]  [              ]    │
│  Age: [  ]  Yrs. School [  ]         Age: [  ]  Yrs. School [  ]      │
│  [ Married        ▼]                 [ Married        ▼]              │
│  Dependents (not listed by Co-Borrower)  Dependents (not listed by Borrower) │
│  no. [  ]  ages [        ]           no. [  ]  ages [        ]        │
│  Present Address:                    Present Address:                 │
│  Street:                             Street:                          │
│  [                      ]            [                      ]          │
│  City:                               City:                            │
│  [                  ]  State:[  ]    [                  ]  State:[  ]  │
│  Zip:                                Zip:                             │
│  [              ]                    [              ]                  │
│                                                                       │
│  [ Rent  ▼]                          [ Rent  ▼]                       │
└─────────────────────────────────────────────────────────────────────┘
```

Part III begins with few challenges, unless you can't remember your name or social security number. However, there are some cautions and helpful insights about the subsequent blocks.

- If you are self-employed, your home phone should not be the same number you list in Part IV as your business phone.

- Lenders are not permitted to discriminate against a borrower because of age. If you don't want to fill in the blank, don't.

- "Years of school" is a quasi-capacity, quasi-character question. The lender is not asking whether or not you earned any degrees, just how many years you attended some kind of school. Don't cheat yourself—there's all kinds of "school" out there. As a corollary, more is not necessarily better.

- Only check the box "Separated" if you are legally separated. Living apart with the intention of being divorced is not inherently the same. If you check this box, be prepared to provide papers that document the division and ownership of property.

- If you are married and want to borrow as an individual in a community property state, your spouse will have to sign a quit claim deed giving up his or her right to title.

- The "Dependents" information should be identical to that on your IRS return.

Information appearing on your loan application will be cross-checked with other documentation you provide. If you have a complicated situation, you must be sure that the information you provide from different sources agrees.

- Although the form has only two additional spaces for past residences, if you move around every few months, even for a good reason, you will probably be asked for more than two previous addresses. The lender would really like to know where you've been the past 7 years, with a minimum verification of 2 years depending on how stable other aspects of your life have been. And if you do provide multiple addresses, be prepared to verify that you paid your rent or mortgage on time for at least the last 2 years.

TRUE STORY: LENDER CHALLENGES INCONSISTENCY

Jack Grisson had a letter of explanation in his credit file about a series of late payments due to expensive medical treatment for his child. On his form, however, he listed no dependents. The lender challenged Jack's loan application: "You have a discrepancy between the information here and on your tax returns from a year ago." The sad fact is that Jack's child had died after a lengthy illness, and it didn't occur to him that he needed to mention that to the lender.

The lender was probing only because of the nature of Jack's explanation of recent credit difficulties. Given the circumstances, it would not have been out of line to require that the death certificate be included in Jack's loan application.

Part IV is straightforward for the salaried person who has been with the same employer for several years doing the same job, or jobs that bear a relationship to each other. If you have become self-employed, or changed jobs and/or employers in recent years, it may be harder for you to convince lenders that you have job stability and consistency, key benchmarks for them in assessing their risk *vis-a-vis* your cash flow to service a mortgage loan.

There are numerous ways that information in this section can trigger scrutiny. Let's take a look at the two main scenarios: a history of employment by others, and a history that includes self-employment.

If you have been consistently employed by others, whether salaried (W-2) or non-salaried (1099), in the subject time frame, at least five items would require explanation:

1. Short periods of employment at different places. You may have a good reason for this, but be prepared to explain it.

IV. Employment Information

Borrower	Co-Borrower
Name & Address of Employer: ☐ Self Employed	Name & Address of Employer: ☐ Self Employed
Street:	Street:
City:	City:
Zip: State:	Zip: State:
☐ Yrs. on this job:	☐ Yrs. on this job:
Yrs. Employed in this line of work/profession: ☐	Yrs. Employed in this line of work/profession: ☐
Position/Title/Type of Business:	Position/Title/Type of Business:
Business Phone:	Business Phone:

If employed in current position for less than two years or if currently employed in more than one position complete the following:

TRUE STORY: LAID OFF AGAIN

Steve Mennarius began his career in marketing with a large computer manufacturer in 1992. Six months later the company downsized and eliminated his job, but his boss remained. Steve went to work for a small software company, but was unhappy with the salary, lack of budget for his department, and work environment. A year later, his old company reorganized again and created a job like the one he had before. His old boss hired him immediately. Six months later—and this story is familiar to people in the computer industry—Steve was laid off again.

His next job involved computers to the extent that everyone had a desktop model, but that was it. He finally got the stability he sought, but all the lender saw at the time of application was a guy who had had four jobs in four years.

Steve got his loan because the nature of his work was consistent in each position, and his explanations of the abrupt changes were supported by reorganization memos that he had saved from the company.

---

2. Several jobs that seem to bear no relationship to each other. In some cases, you just didn't like what you were doing, so you sought a more fulfilling opportunity. That could satisfy a lender if the most recent position involves a substantial salary increase, and/or ties in with an educational or training program that has put you on a career track, for example. Then again, there are cases in which it is not obvious that there is a relationship between one job and another. Explain the link, but do it in terms the lender will understand.

TRUE STORY: REVEALING THE CONSISTENCY

Margaret O'Malley worked her way through graduate school by maintaining a job as an office manager at a small investment banking firm. At the firm, she had daily exposure to budgets, P&Ls, and other financial instruments, and hands-on experience with the operation of a business. Armed with that knowledge as well as her new master's degree in theater arts, she landed a job as Managing Director of a small theater. Two years later, the frustration of being underpaid and overworked drove her to accept a job doing corporate fundraising for a major museum in New York. She had a lot of explaining to do when she attempted to buy a home later that year.

Margaret got her loan because she demonstrated that, in each case, she built on her skill sets, increased her salary, and got more focused about using her business acumen in an arts-related profession.

---

3. Titles that seem to indicate a loss of stature in a profession. Common sense does not apply here, because if it did, a lender would recognize that corporate titles are often meaningless. (One Silicon Valley company employs "software evangelists.") Again, you need to point out tactfully why your titles don't mean that you got less and less competent.

TRUE STORY: WHAT'S IN A TITLE?

Larry Wu started consulting for computer systems right after graduation from Stanford. His first job title was "President, Wu Systems Experts." Larry made himself so valuable to one of his clients that the company offered him a third more than he was earning on his own; he came to work as "Director, Computer Systems." His next move a year later was to a giant computer company, where he held the generic title "Manager."

Larry made more than twice as much as a manager as he did as a president, with the prospect of moving up through the ranks at a company with a global presence and thousands of employees.

If you have been self-employed, even if you are currently employed by someone else, keep in mind the same cautions on job consistency and time period as with a salaried person.

In addition, if you are self-employed items that are inappropriate or would require explanation include:

4. A business phone that is the same as the home phone. Before filing your application, allocate separate lines for business and personal use if you work out of your house, and be sure your business line has the proper listing with directory assistance.

5. A short period of self-employment exists between salaried jobs. When a lender sees this, it appears you are disguising an employment gap by calling it a period of self-employment. It is highly likely that a lender will ask for your tax returns in that case, so you have to be able to substantiate your claim.

True Story: Lenders Play Detective

Randy Ponce had a legitimate reason for an employment gap. A loan officer convinced him it was better to write an explanatory letter than cover up the gap with a self-employment entry.

Randy's letter measured up in every way except one. He indicated that he left his job to follow his wife, Nancy, to a different state so she could take an excellent position in her field. Unfortunately, the lender happened to notice that Randy's co-borrower and wife was Betty, so the lender asked for a copy of the divorce decree, as well as tax returns to ensure there were no dependents, child support payments or alimony inadvertently omitted from the loan application.

Parts V and VI

Before examining Part V, here are important reminders for self-employed people: If you want a no income stated loan, then do not fill in the boxes requesting income. If you are going for a quick qualifier package, be sure to list your gross income. That is, if you bring in $15,000 a month, and have $5,000 in expenses, list the $15,000. The lender will deduct your expenses from income to determine a net figure.

V. MONTHLY INCOME AND COMBINED HOUSING EXPENSE INFORMATION

Gross Monthly Income	Borrower	Co-Borrower
Base Employment Income*	$	$
Overtime		
Bonuses		
Commissions		
Dividends/Interest		
Net Rental Income:		
Other		
Total		

*Self Employed Borrower(s) may be required to provide additional documentation such as tax returns and financial statements.

Contingencies such as these dominate Part V. The following are key examples:

- If you are salaried and any portion your annual income comes from overtime, bonuses, or commissions, then you must provide a letter from your employer stating the likelihood of its continuance.

- If any portion of your annual income flows from investments, then you must provide documentation of the likelihood of its continuance. Be careful about not double-counting investment income that you have earmarked for part of your down payment.

- If you have rental income, then you have to complete Part VI and use the "Net Rental Income" number here. After you complete Part VI, the lender will apply the standard formula to determine the net income for purposes of your loan:

  Gross Rental income – 25 percent – PITI = Net Rental Income.

 If your expenses on the property are less than 25 percent of the rental you charge, you have to prove it to supersede the default calculation. Be prepared through Schedule E of your tax returns to show the lender why the standard formula doesn't apply.

On the "Monthly Housing Expense" side, it is in your best interest to be forthcoming about all your housing expenses. If you rent garage space in addition to a home, for example, include that cost in your monthly rental figure. Lenders contrast your current monthly housing expenses with your proposed monthly mortgage payment to judge whether or not you are likely to have payment shock with the forthcoming loan. Too big a difference—and this is a somewhat subjective measure—could make a lender reluctant to approve a loan at the level requested.

The simplistic advice for Part VI is "Go as high as possible with assets and as low as possible with liabilities." *Liquid assets* are cash and investments you can immediately turn into cash. Other assets include real estate, cars, and the original Van Gogh hanging in your living room. In the liabilities section, you can say, "See credit report." This will help you avert the mistake of overstating your liabilities.

In the space requesting the name of the entity holding your cash deposit toward the purchase, that is, your down payment, enter the name of the escrow company or other institutional third-party that has your cash.

PARTS VII AND VIII

VII. DETAILS OF TRANSACTION	
(a) Purchase price:	$
(b) Alterations, improvements, repairs:	$
(c) Land (if acquired separately):	$
(d) Refinance (incl. debts to be paid off):	$
(e) Estimated prepaid items:	$
(f) Estimated closing costs:	$
(g) PMI, MIO, Funding Fee:	$
(h) Discount (if Borrower will pay):	$
(i) Total Costs (add items a through h):	$
(j) Subordinate financing:	$
(k) Borrower's closing costs paid by Seller:	$
(l) Other Credits Explain:	$
(m) Loan amount (exlude items from line g):	$
(n) PMI, MIP, Funding Fee financed:	$
(o) Loan amount (add m & n)	$
(p) Cash from/to Borrower (subtract j, k, l & o from i):	$

In Part VII, you and the lender work together closely to express the details of your costs. This is not the same as letting the lender take over. It is important you that understand the layers of charges that make up final numbers such as estimated *prepaid items* and estimated *closing costs*, fees and charges paid at the end of a real estate transaction. The former would include items paid out of pocket, like appraisal and credit report fees. The latter would include processing and document delivery charges. Chapter 9 addresses in detail the legitimate costs and *garbage fees* you can face at closing.

Just as Parts I through VII focus on areas the lender wants to examine to be financially protected, the final sections bring certain legal considerations into play. They are what you might call CYA ("cover your assets") questions and instructions: In many cases the information requested here and statements to which are you asked to attest have appeared in other forms in the previous sections. This is your last chance to tell the truth again, or hang yourself with an inconsistency or deception.

The following are interpretations that will help you answer every declaration in Part VIII truthfully. Refer to Appendix A, the full loan, or the application at the www.maze.com Web site for a point-by-point reference.

a. "Are there any outstanding judgments against you?" might have required a "yes" at the beginning of your application process back at the start of the Mortgage Maze. In the meantime, however, you have satisfied outstanding debts in order to qualify for a loan. The answer to the question, then, is probably "no." If it isn't, you have a lot of explaining to do.

b. If you have declared bankruptcy within the past seven years, add a continuation sheet that specifies what kind, what caused it, when you paid off the debts that caused your bankruptcy (or when you will), and how you have reorganized your finances since that time.

c. During the 1980s, in several areas of the country, property values sunk far below the mortgage amount. It became somewhat common for people to avoid foreclosure by giving the lender the deed "in lieu of" foreclosure. Basically, the lender would rent the property for the payment amount, and the borrower escaped a dead-end mortgage arrangement without facing foreclosure and/or bankruptcy. An explanatory letter sheds light on the exact circumstances, the most critical of which may be a depressed real estate market.

d. A "yes" to "Are you party to a lawsuit?" can cause problems whether you are the plaintiff or defendant. This is because, even if you are the one suing for damages, you have to make it clear what your potential liability is if you are counter-sued.

e. Be very careful that you tell the truth (as usual) on the question about other loan obligations. Not all loans show up on your credit report, but failing to report all loans is viewed as an attempt to defraud the lender. Even if you know, for example, that your Small Business Administration (SBA) loan is so small that the SBA does not report it, you must. If your omission is discovered, all arrangements stop immediately and you are in hot water with the law.

f. The same guidance given in *e.* above applies here.

g. You have been asked the question about alimony and child support in several ways by this time. If you've managed to hide your payments in the previous sections, and escaped having your tax returns reviewed, this declaration is one final reminder that you have to confess.

h. Again, you have been asked this question about your available cash before, but not in so straightforward a manner. Think about it.

i. Have you co-signed on an education loan for your son or daughter? Did you ever help a friend get a loan? Even if the person you helped has assumed full responsibility for the payments, your name is still on the note and you need to explain how big your potential liability is, and when the obligation will end.

j. and k. are self-explanatory. What a relief!

l. If you have the intention of occupying the property, the answer is "yes." Lenders know that circumstances often change later— separation and divorce are common reasons—but on this form you express your plans at the moment.

m. Again, this is a straightforward question. Either you owned all or part of a property in the past 3 years, or you didn't.

Part IX

Following is an examination of each phrase in Part IX:

1. The loan and the property must match. The lender is protecting itself against fraud relating to a loan for a non-existent property.

2. The property should not be an opium den or house of ill repute (except in Nevada, where "ill repute" does not necessarily mean "illegal.").

3. This loan application should correspond to the loan in question. It is not appropriate to "white out" certain answers and resubmit a signed application to another entity for another loan.

4. If you say you're going to live in the property, you're supposed to mean it. Similarly, if you say the property is a second home or investment, you are expected to abide by those rules of occupancy. Your honest intention regarding occupancy may be different from the reality because of changing circumstances; document your reasons for the change in case the lender challenges you.

5. Your loan will most likely be sold in the secondary market, with certain rights regarding verification of your assertions assigned to another party. In this clause, the lender asserts the right to retain the original copy of your application—reports, letters, signatures, and any other documentation.

6. While the loan application is a snapshot of your financial situation at a particular moment, if that moment is early in the process, and any "material fact" of your financial situation has changed by the time you are near closing, you promise here that you will amend your application accordingly. For example, if your teenaged dependent causes your neighbor's arrest by planting marijuana in the backyard, your potential liability is high and you must amend your loan application with the pertinent facts.

7. You give up your rights to privacy about your mortgage delinquencies in this clause.

8. You give the lender the right to sell your loan and to transfer the ability to *service the loan*, that is handle the ongoing administrative aspects of the loan. This does not give the lender or servicing company the right to change the terms of the loan, however.

9. The lender may be giving you money to buy a property, but is not giving you any assurances that the property is physically sound, marketable, pesticide free, or harboring good karma.

The Certification clause merely asks you, one more time, to attest to the fact that the application contains the truth.

 Be sure that the signatures on the application for borrower and co-borrower are the same as those on other documents bearing the names of both. Do not have a spouse or secretary sign your name to expedite the process.

In the Maze Master's opinion . . .
Part IX is going to keep growing. The "Acknowledgment and Agreement" section preceding your signature has expanded over time to encompass more and more promises. And when the size of the paragraph gets larger but the paper doesn't, the type gets smaller. That's important because, as you may know, in legal documents the big print giveth, and the small print taketh away.

PART X

Don't misconstrue the purpose of Section X! It is, as it says, for government monitoring purposes. Lenders have an obligation by law to distribute funds in accordance with their depositor base. In other words, if the Main Street branch of Bank Q gets 90 percent of its deposits from Hispanic customers, that bank is legally obligated to allocate a comparable amount of mortgage loan money to Hispanic people. It is absolutely wrong to think that this part of the application sets you up for discrimination—quite the contrary. Fill in the blanks on race and national origin honestly. You may be eligible for a Community Reinvestment Act (CRA) loan or other special loan packages tied to zip code, census tract, or national origin.

With application in hand, and a good sense of your borrowing power, you are now ready to scrutinize the lender.

Chapter 7

A Bigger Intersection:
Select a Lender

Selecting the right lender saves a buyer the time and aggravation of dealing with a "no," a hundred unnecessary requests that still lead to "no," the prospect of terms that are onerous, or a lender of questionable stability. Fundamentally, you need to know which lender does which type of loan better than another.

You need to choose a lender or lending institution who will serve you, the client, rather than the other way around. You need to know when to shop for rates, and when to shop for terms. Shopping for rates when terms should be the focus will complicate the Mortgage Maze. You can follow a clear path through the selection process.

TYPES OF LENDERS

The two main types of lenders are those that accept deposits and those that don't, that is, *institutional lenders* and *non-institutional lenders*. The former are inter- and intra-state banks, certain securities firms, savings and loans (including thrifts), and credit unions. Among the non-institutional lenders are *mortgage bankers*, pension funds, and private lenders. Some mortgage brokers also fund loans through a special arrangement with a bank. A third, non-traditional lender is a person, like a relative or friend, who does not make loans as part of a business.

INSTITUTIONAL LENDERS

The most common types of institutional lenders are banks and S&Ls. At one time, most of these lending institutions had loan committees, with each member of the committee evaluating and rendering a judgment on pending loan applications. Some small banks still use this model, but larger institutions tend to entrust a single individual with signature authority, at least to a certain loan dollar amount.

A typical flow of paperwork within the large institution would be from a *loan processor*, who ensures that the proper documents are in the borrower's file and in order, to a *first-line underwriter*, or first-signature underwriter, who might be able to approve up to $150,000, or perhaps $300,000 or more, depending on the bank. If the loan amount exceeds the first-line underwriter's authority, or the package has quirks that the underwriter would like another pair of eyes to examine, that person would send it on to a colleague. The message would be, "I recommend approving this at the limit requested," or "I recommend approving this subject to satisfactorily documenting x, y, and z." The first underwriter might wait until receiving that documentation to pass the package on to a higher authority; the second underwriter may either approve the loan or be required to send it to a still higher authority. At each level, the underwriter might add conditions for approval and stop the process until the conditions are met.

Most large lending institutions have a rule-of-thumb about approvals of strong loan packages: It takes one to approve, but at least two to decline.

The role of the mortgage broker in the approval mechanism, whether the loan application is going to an institutional lender or a mortgage banker, is to assume responsibility for the loan processing, find the best loan, and get approval of that loan, or approval after certain conditions are met. The broker is supposed to minimize your headaches and reduce your confusion from beginning to end of the maze. In terms of your packaging, going to a broker is like going to a professional resumé writer.

Choosing one institutional lender instead of another involves two major considerations: First, your knowledge of what the market offers and second your leverage with a particular lender. This book gives you countless hints on what kind of information you need about the market. But when it comes to leverage, unless you have tremendous assets in lots of different places, you don't have a control over who your lender will be. For example, you simply will not have influence when accessing the lending services of Wall Street investment firms and major banks if you do not have substantial investment portfolios with them that you have maintained for several years. Even then, despite the fact that they profess to make it easy for their preferred clients to get a mortgage loan, the paperwork demands and qualifying standards are generally so high, you may not want to go that route unless your loan amount exceeds $650,000 (a level of loan often referred to as *super jumbo*). These companies have one set of guidelines and requirements for all applicants. For very high loan amounts, Wall Street firms' requirements may actually be less cumbersome than their institutional competitors. In addition, the pricing on these large loans is generally better, that is, the rate and terms are more desirable.

Recall the story of Carmine Longwood in Chapter 6. In the aftermath, he decided to investigate his rejection by the securities firm that held a $6 million investment portfolio that he managed. In doing so, he discovered that the loan officer for the securities firm had never even contacted Carmine's account representative in investments. He was going strictly "by the ratios" when he rejected the loan application. When Carmine insisted he contact the account rep, the loan officer discovered that the company was making about $18,000 a month on Carmine's portfolio. When that fact was known, it dramatically changed his leverage with the firm!

While leverage or the influence of your asset-based relationship with an institutional lender can be key to getting a desirable deal, the familiarity of a lender with your assets can be a double-edged sword. You may think your long-standing status as a depositor strengthens your position, but because you've done business there a long time, the institution also has access to more years of your financial history than you may want to involve in your application.

Throughout the loan application process, keep as much control as possible over your financial information. Respond completely to the lender's specific requests, but don't volunteer information. Do not put yourself in a situation where a lender can quickly and completely "undress" you. In a way, you might want to think of this as one of your "rights of the road" in the Mortgage Maze.

Just as a lender examines you to determine risk, you might want to assess the stability of the lending institution, especially if you also have a depository relationship with the lender. As a depositor, you are lending your money to the institution and want assurances that you will get it back. As a borrower, while your primary interests are getting the best loan and good customer service, knowing that the financial community thinks highly of your bank might be an important corollary for you. If your lending institution should collapse, however, your loan and its terms would remain the same while an oversight agency, such as the Office of Thrift Supervision (OTS), picks up the portfolio and transfers it to another institution for servicing.

It is easy to satisfy your curiosity about the stability of your bank. While the *Federal Deposit Insurance Corporation (FDIC)* which oversees banks does not release its ratings on the safety and soundness of institutions to the public, there are private companies that do provide the service to consumers through publications and over the phone. Without endorsement of their evaluations, the FDIC lists the following private sources of information about institutional lenders at its web site.

Private Sources of Information About Institutional Lenders

Publications.
Bank Financial Quarterly and *S&L-Savings Bank Financial Quarterly* (IDC Financial Publishing, 800-525-5457). The first book rates commercial banks and bank holding companies; the latter rates S&Ls

and savings banks. Listings show a rank on a scale of 300 (best) to 1 for each institution.

The Bank Quarterly, Ratings and Analysis and *The S&L Quarterly, Ratings and Analysis* (Sheshunoff Information Services, 800-456-2340). The first book rates commercial banks and savings banks, while the second rates all FDIC-insured S&Ls. Listings show a rank on a scale of 99 (best) to 1 for each institution.

Quarterly Bank and S&L Rating Service (Lace Financial, 301-662-1011). Rankings from A+ to E cover FDIC-insured banks and S&Ls.

Ratings by Phone.
Bauer Group (800-388-6686) provides financial highlights and ratings on all federally-insured banks, S&Ls and credit unions.

IDC Financial (800-525-5457) delivers a rating and a written report on any federally-insured bank, bank holding company, S&L, or credit union.

Veribanc (800-442-2657 or 800-837-4226) gives you ratings on any federally-insured bank, S&L, or credit union.

Call the services for current prices, which range from a couple dollars to about $25, depending on whether or not you want a written report.

NON-INSTITUTIONAL LENDERS

Many union members, such as carpenters and longshoremen, have money in a pension fund that makes mortgage loans. Some of these, such as the State Teachers Retirement System (STRS), lend to members of the retirement group who are retired or currently working and contributing to their fund. Similarly, the Public Employees Retirement System (PERS) restricts its lending to active members. As part of their loan package PERS members must document their ongoing contributions to the retirement fund. The pension fund for the Carpenters Union even lends money to builders who use 100 percent union labor. If you are one of the few people who has access to mortgage money through your pension fund, use the qualification and application guidelines in this book to help you package yourself and negotiate. If you present yourself well, you will probably find it is possible for you to get a better rate, as well as more palatable terms and conditions through your group than with an institutional lender. The process should be less of a struggle, too.

TRUE STORY: UNLOCKING A HIGHER INTEREST RATE

Billy Border locked his loan with his pension fund just before rates fell substantially. He went back to his pension fund to ask if his rate could be lowered even though he had agreed to a higher rate with the lock. The loan officer accommodated him and added an insight that made Billy feel great. The loan officer admitted that out of the 17 loans recently funded, Billy's was the only one that got a lower rate. If he hadn't asked, he would have been stuck up there with the other 16 borrowers.

The moral is, "Stay current with the market, and never be afraid to ask for a better deal." Lenders won't necessarily compromise after a lock, but might consider it if the rate has fallen $\frac{1}{4}$ to $\frac{3}{8}$ of a percent.

More commonly, if a borrower goes to a non-institutional lender, it is a mortgage banker. Mortgage bankers are middlemen. After they sign off on loans, they fund the loan with money borrowed from lines of credit from banks and/or other sources. After closing, they immediately sell the loans to Fannie Mae, Freddie Mac, Wall Street firms, or other institutions and investors. Many times mortgage bankers also sell to other mortgage bankers, who are master sellers for securities firms or pension funds.

Mortgage bankers may offer a better rate than the bank because they operate with lower overhead. They focus on the resulting margin and don't care so much about physical image as a bank.

Investor approval can play a pivotal role in dealing with a mortgage banker, and it can mean a couple things. It can mean that the loan is going to be underwritten by the institution that will ultimately buy the loan. Another possibility is that a mortgage insurance company, or other third party, will underwrite it. This is the most likely possibility if the loan is destined for a Wall Street security firm. If that's the case, your package had better be A-1, because these third-party underwriters are rigid in their adherence to guidelines and reliance on artificial intelligence, such as credit scoring, mortgage scoring and bankruptcy scoring.

On occasion, mortgage brokers can also become lenders through a special arrangement with a lending institution. The process called table funding is an incentive to the brokerage to focus its loan volume on that particular institution. By giving the broker the ability to fund in the name of the firm, with the loan moving immediately to the bank or S&L after the ink is dry on the documents, that lending institution makes it possible for the broker to earn higher fees. This does not necessarily mean that you, the borrower, get a less desirable deal, however. The broker may well offer you a bargain basement rate due to the special relationship with the lender that makes table funding possible. You may pay a few extra dollars in fees, but your long-term benefits could be impressive.

The rules of the game can become more idiosyncratic when private lenders get involved. If you have a strange or strained situation that makes it hard to get approval from other lenders, you could ask your real estate agent and mortgage broker if they know of private sources of mortgage money.

A private lender is a person with money who takes a chance on a high risk case. It is that person's money. A mortgage banker loans someone else's money.

Private loans are often used to cure a first loan or to provide enough cash to the borrower to clear up delinquencies. A private lender might want to get involved if the subject property has appreciated substantially since you got the first mortgage and it is highly marketable. Needless to say, since your late mortgage payments, property tax payments, and the like make you unsatisfactory to other lenders, you cannot expect the private source to be kind about rates or terms.

Non-Traditional Lenders

By their nature, non-traditional lenders are a one-time source of funds. They are relatives, friends, or other people who believe in you and are not in the business of financing home purchases. Here, character rules.

Personal sources such as these, of course, may or may not expect repayment of the loan in a traditional manner. They may or may not want interest. They may or may not want an equity stake in your home. One arrangement is an equity partnership: Grandma wants to recoup what she put into your house but also a little more, an "equity kicker," at some point in time or upon the profitable sale of the property.

Going this route sounds easy, doesn't it? It is. It means you are flying over the maze instead of navigating it.

Lenders' Objectives

The lenders' primary objectives for granting mortgages shape the different grades and types of loans that are available to you. The pair of mutually reinforcing objectives that all lenders share is the desire to sustain profitability and reduce costs. In addition, most lenders have an overriding aim to make mortgages as risk-free as possible. There are some, however, that will assume increased risk in exchange for a higher profit margin.

For those who want to minimize risk in all cases, artificial intelligence plays a major role. A tool of growing importance to these lenders is credit scoring and *bankruptcy scoring*. Credit scoring, which was covered in Chapter 3, begins by assigning a high score, then removing points for flaws in your payment performance, types and amount of credit accounts, and so on. Bankruptcy scoring, such as that prepared by a company like CCN-MDS, begins with a low score, then add points for bad behavior in an effort to predict the likelihood of your declaring bankruptcy.

In a 1995 letter to CEOs and credit officers of all its sellers and servicers, Freddie Mac stressed "the predictive power of selected credit scores." The letter stated,

> Freddie Mac studied how hundreds of thousands of loans performed over several years to determine which attributes of the loan

file were most predictive of default. We identified a strong correlation between mortgage performance and two types of credit scores, created by national credit scoring companies and frequently used in consumer lending. The types of credit scores we reviewed were 'bureau scores,' as prepared by Fair, Isaac and Co., Inc. (FICO) and 'bankruptcy scores,' as prepared by CCN-MDS (MDS).

The chart below illustrates the predictive power of these credit scores:

FREDDIE MAC SCORING GUIDELINES

If the FICO bureau score is	or the MDS bankruptcy score is	then the recommended approach to reviewing credit is
over 660	less than 550	BASIC: Underwrite the file as required to confirm the borrower's willingness to repay as agreed.
660 to 620	550 to 700	COMPREHENSIVE: Underwrite all aspects of the borrower's credit history to establish the borrower's willingness to repay as agreed.
less than 620	over 700	CAUTIOUS: Perform a particularly detailed review of all aspects of the borrower's credit history to ensure that you have satisfactorily established the borrower's willingness to repay as agreed. Unless there are extenuating circumstances, a credit score in this range should be viewed as a strong indication that the borrower does not show sufficient willingness to repay as agreed.

MDS BANKRUPTCY SCORE

No numbers on the percentage of defaults have been provided on the chart. This is part of the "secret stuff" that the scoring companies hold closely.

In order to understand how the lender's objective of making risk-free loans affects your options, look at the guidelines below from Freddie Mac that were also provided in the 1995 letter. Freddie Mac prefaces its notes with the stern suggestion: "For 1-unit single-family dwellings, we suggest that you apply the information in the following chart before underwriting borrower creditworthiness as required . . ."

Here is the Maze Master's interpretation of Freddie Mac's chart:

If the FICO bureau score is	or the MDS bankruptcy score is	then the recommended approach to reviewing credit is
over 660	less than 550	Underwrite the file because the score proves that the borrower has no need for the money anyway. This borrower can go anywhere.
660 to 620	550 to 700	Place conditions on the loan; make the borrower verify everything. If you can get a higher down payment than the one being offered, go ahead.
less than 620	over 700	Fat chance.

In this book, the fact that there is a loan for virtually everyone with decent collateral is a fundamental message. How can that be reconciled with the caution, on the basis of artificial intelligence, to eliminate anyone with a deficient score as a loan candidate? As you will soon see, *how* different lenders choose to achieve their objectives of sustaining profitability and reducing costs gives rise to programs for relatively high-risk borrowers. There is a loan for virtually everyone, but sometimes it is at a price that you don't want to pay unless you're desperate. If you are desperate, think of yourself as going 90 mph through the maze and hitting slippery pavement on a turn. You might make it through, but then again, you might crash.

Large banks, small banks and S&Ls all have slightly different agendas when it comes to mortgages. Large banks generally make home loans available because they want to draw depositors, build a servicing portfolio, and originate mortgages for sales in the secondary market. Small banks also want to draw depositors, but are less interested in servicing mortgages. Their objective is to roll mortgage money as many times in a year as possible. They can be tough lenders because their eyes are always on the secondary market. S&Ls look for a higher yield on mortgages and do want to build servicing portfolios with customers that can be both borrowers and depositors. They are a likely source of mortgages for people with problems who are willing to pay a premium. You might find them almost human in their decision making.

And, as you might have guessed, an objective of the Wall Street firms in entering a market traditionally dominated by the banks and S&Ls is to attract large securities accounts. Give them your millions, and they will be happy to give you their millions, for a small fee. Wall Street firms are really high-class mortgage bankers. Whereas a mortgage banker is a middleman or a pass-through for mortgages going straight to Wall Street, the Wall Street firms that lend mortgage money cut out the middleman. The difference becomes which entity puts your loan through the computerized scoring and other artificial intelligence tests that deem it securitizable.

DIFFERENT LENDERS, DIFFERENT TERMS

The streets used to be filled with benevolent lenders with the word "yes" forming on their lips as you walked through the front door. Not so any more, which means that some target only the lowest-risk borrower with their loan programs, and others are in the higher-margin business of serving relatively high-risk borrowers. A few lending institutions try to do both. Regardless of their approach, the lenders are all trying to originate mortgages that will create a positive cash flow with the least amount of trouble.

GRADES OF LOANS

Loans are graded A through D with A being the best grade (least expensive) and D being the lowest (the most expensive). So far, the packaging tips and cautions to get you through the Mortgage Maze efficiently have prepared you to get an A loan. As you saw in the Freddie Mac recommendations, however, the role of artificial intelligence in the underwriting process may simply knock you out of contention for the most desirable product. If you do have a score or other factors that limit your options, try to move past the obstacle and toward the best loan. Having done that, if you don't qualify for the best loan, establish parameters for what you will accept and know how long it will take to upgrade your situation. When the lender tells you what the offer is, make sure you understand the rates, terms (especially prepayment terms), and costs.

Never enter the Mortgage Maze with your sights on anything less than an A loan. After you present yourself in the best light and still find out you don't qualify for the best rates and ideal terms, then explore other options. Lenders make a premium by down-grading loans made to medium- or high-risk borrowers. If you are a marginal case, do not assume that you are powerless to push yourself into the A category. Shop around, and seek help from a mortgage professional.

Here are the different grades of loans and some characteristics. With the A loan you have a reliable car on a smooth highway. It is usually a strong loan package, but not necessarily perfect. Any bumps in the road have been avoided or seamlessly patched by nego-tiating with the lender, credit grantor, or reporting source, and it is immediately salable and securitizable. The four Cs, capacity, credit, collateral, and character, are self-evident in the A loan.

With the A– ("A minus") loan you have a decent car on a gener-ally good road. There are a few imperfections in the road, and some evidence of patching, that make navigating the maze slightly more difficult. Strong compensating factors are evident; there is not a completely desirable borrower profile. This becomes an A loan with a little seasoning, that is, 6 months to a year of regular payments as agreed. The borrower pays a premium, so it is slightly more expen-sive than the A loan, and with good explanations of problems and a few adjustments, a portfolio lender might do as an A loan. In some cases, it could have become an A loan with better presentation. In the Mortgage Maze, how you look on paper is "who you are," that is, your presentation is your reality.

With the B loan your bad tires make you feel insecure as you go over the bumps. A B loan sometimes results from the borrower's laziness in not providing solid explanations for late payments and other credit problems. Known deficiencies in the borrower's profile make the loan unmarketable in its early months, but paying the loan as agreed can lead to an upgrade. The lender is betting on this happening.

The B loan requires longer seasoning than the A loan for mar-ketability, so the borrower pays a premium with a higher down payment (lower LTV). This loan may be moved from servicing to collections as early as the second late payment. It can be sold to the secondary market, but only after a guarantee from the originating lender for a period of time after seasoning.

In the representations and warranties (called "reps and warranties") that the lender makes on a low-grade loan, the lender commits to taking the package back for at least the first 90 days, and perhaps even during the first 2 years if problems arise. Sometimes in the case of early default, though, the lender does have the ability to substitute a comparable or better loan in the portfolio. The reserve requirements associated with representations and warranties are so stringent that the lender invariably charges the borrower a premium up front in fees and may tack on a stiff prepayment penalty. Many low-grade loans are held by the lender until they no longer require reps and warranties because of the reserve requirements.

With the C loan your old car that needs work to pass inspection is giving you a scary ride along a winding, bumpy road. Usually, the borrower's credit report displays current past-dues, collection accounts, and liens that need to be paid in escrow.

If you dispute a lien on your property or item on your credit report, the lender may allow you to put 150 percent of the then-current amount of the debt in escrow until the dispute is resolved, rather than compel you to pay the credit grantor. The lender normally puts a time limit on this arrangement, and joint instructions are issued by you and the lender to the escrow company on how to handle the money. They could involve returning the money or paying the disputed items at some designated time in the future. If you must put money in escrow, ask that it go into an interest-bearing account.

Deficiencies in the borrower's profile make the C loan unmarketable in its early months, and possibly not at all. It requires seasoning of at least 24 months with a perfect payment record. The borrower pays a premium, so it is more expensive that the B loan, approaching "we're going to stick it to you" rates and fees. The lender protects itself with a lower LTV, and the C loan will be collected as soon as the first late payment.

Collecting a loan is different from servicing a loan, which involves gentle and courteous treatment from a lender who respects your A status and understands that you might be late because you are traveling abroad. Collecting a loan entails reminder calls from your lender, probably starting on the 3rd of the month, despite the fact that your grace period for paying as agreed extends to the 10th or even 15th. Don't confuse the payment due-date with the end of the grace period, or you'll often be late!

If your loan application rates a D loan, your clunker is running out of gas on a rocky, winding road and heavy rains have obscured your vision as you look for the last on-ramp to the highway. The D loan is referred to as an "asset only" loan because it sure isn't your credit history or character that convinces a lender to do business with you. This loan changes hands only if the FDIC or OTS takes over the institution and picks it up. The borrower pays a premium, so it is slightly more expensive than the C loan, and you've arrived at "we're sticking it to you" rates. Expect the lowest LTV, usually 40 to 65 percent.

The D loan amounts are a maximum of $350,000 to $400,000 and requires strong collateral. The lender who makes this loan might want to own your house and will probably require two appraisals by the actual lender. The D loan normally bails you out of default or pays off someone who is about to take your first born.

True Story: Expensive Bail-Outs

Phillip Morgan got a D loan in 1992, after he narrowly escaped foreclosure on his previous property. Over the next couple years, his situation stabilized considerably. He was getting good performance reviews at work, where he had been employed for nearly two decades. Due to a protracted divorce proceeding, however, he felt vulnerable in the face of a lender's scrutiny and took the "easy route" (what an oxymoron) when he refinanced: He got another D loan.

Phillip could have upgraded if he had shopped around. Instead, in a market with fixed interest rates at around 7.5 percent, he was paying 15.25 percent!

His plight got worse. Not only did Phillip fall two payments behind and need another bail-out, but his property had also depreciated substantially and the bail-out to pay off the current loan was going to cost him a $6,900 prepayment penalty.

Most private lenders use D parameters in making loans. Because many of them have gotten stuck with property, particularly in the early- to mid-1990s, they will apply "stick it to you" rates and terms, as well as enforce heavy appraisal requirements and inspect the property personally.

An ARM provides a good example of how B through D lenders use rates and terms to increase their profitability in exchange for higher perceived risk. The standard A and A– loan will have an adjustment every 6 months to a year with a 1 percent to 2 percent adjustment cap, respectively. It will also have a reasonable life cap of 5 or 6 percent over the start rate. On the other hand, B through D lenders often try to lull the troubled borrower into thinking he or she is getting a good deal by offering an attractive teaser rate, only to follow it with shocking increases.

Since you are considering such a loan only because you have a spotty, dirty, or thoroughly ugly financial record, you may be desperate enough to perceive the 3- or 6-month teaser rate as part of a desirable product. Look carefully at the loan terms that follow the teaser period! You might find a lower-grade ARM following a teaser period with a 1.5 percent adjustment after only 6 months, and every 6 months thereafter, and have a high interest rate cap or high payment cap. You may also find you face a higher late penalty and shorter grace period. In this case, the light at the end of the tunnel could well be an oncoming train.

Lenders who make B through D loans also tend to make monthly calls to ensure that you don't forget to make your payment on time. The first of the month, you'll get a friendly message from Jamie Smith at the bank who says, "Just a courtesy call to remind you about your mortgage payment!" The calls will continue. The theory is that, after a year or so, you are so uncomfortable hearing from Jamie Smith on the first of the month that you will automatically be prompt in making your payment. This reminds the Maze Master of the story of the baby elephant. When he was small, the circus owner tied him to a stake driven 12 inches into the ground. The baby elephant could only go the 3-foot length of the rope, then the stake would stop him. Finally, even though the elephant grew larger and could have pulled out the stake and run away, he didn't. It didn't occur to him that he could.

Cautions about how B through D lenders do business are not meant to be disparaging. They are business institutions providing a financial service that people want. They take high risk and, if they calculate well, make comparable profits. That risk is like the sword of Damocles, however: At any moment, its weight could be too much for the hair that holds it safely overhead.

PORTFOLIO LOANS

A portfolio loan reflects a lender's desire to establish and maintain a person-to-person relationship which may be tied to your large deposits, or perhaps a relative's. The lender sees logical reasons to make the loan, but you simply don't fit the "A" guidelines. Therefore, before giving you money, the lender will look hard at your collateral and capacity to repay and will examine your character more closely than other lenders. The price you pay for the lender's personal attention is a more expensive loan. The advantage you get is a loan that cures your financial ills or gives you a chance to own a house that, under standard terms, would have been out of your grasp. Despite your unusual circumstances, you get a decent home loan.

In short, portfolio loans have special features or involve special exceptions that enable an unconventional borrower to qualify for a mortgage loan. The following two examples illustrate sample terms and conditions. World S&L, based in Oakland, California, will provide 100 percent financing, with no mortgage insurance for owner-occupied purchases only. You can get different terms, ARM, fixed-rate, and so on, but the firm condition is that you or your sponsors put up or pledge extra collateral in the form of a certificate of deposit (CD) equal to 25 percent of the property value. If you needed only 95 percent financing, you or your sponsor(s) would be expected to buy a CD equal to 20 percent of the property value. The S&L allows up to three CD sponsors. The CD is released once 75 percent of the LTV is reached, based on the original appraisal. There are a few other requirements, but this unusual loan carries A loan pricing and there are other variations out there.

Another portfolio loan, with far less desirable pricing, involves numerous exceptions to the rules but operates on a 3.25 percent margin in a market where the standard for ARMs is 2.5 percent. The person drawn to this loan by circumstance would be paying substantially more than with the World S&L portfolio loan. Nevertheless, if the resources are not available to qualify for a better option, and the property you want warrants concessions on your part, you still become a home owner.

Review for a moment how many different types of loans are out there. You have four major options—fixed, ARM, FIRM, and balloon. You could either have a fully amortizing or a negatively amortizing loan. Your amortization period could be 15, 20, 30 or 40 years. Your ARM could be tied to different margins and indexes. And, if you have problems, they can be cured by a number of different grades of loans. Knowing this, you can be fairly certain that a lender will say "yes" to you eventually. If you are in the position of facing a "no," don't be too concerned. A lender's or a mortgage insurance company's refusal to approve your loan does not mean "Leave the Mortgage Maze!" It is merely a detour sign.

Chapter 8

A Detour: Turn Rejection into an Opportunity

True stories of real people navigating the Mortgage Maze reveal the range of problems that force you to take a detour. Understanding the types of unpleasant surprises that can occur will alert you to any unusual aspect of your financial picture or collateral, and prepare you for critical predicaments that can occur between the conditional approval of your loan and closing.

AN APPROVAL IS JUST AN ON-RAMP

Most first-time home buyers have a hard time believing their real estate agent or mortgage broker about last-minute obstacles to loan approval. It just doesn't seem logical. You have compiled your documentation of assets and liabilities, completed your application, answered a rash of prying questions, and submitted documentation to back up documentation. You are inclined to think it is sadism that drives someone to say that it is still possible for the lender who has conditionally approved your loan to say "no" minutes before closing. Believe it! Count on running into road construction when you are minutes away from your destination, then be delightfully surprised if you don't.

When you get a conditional approval, or approval of your loan "subject to" certain items being turned in or actions being taken, the requirement for more information could come at any, or all, times. If the lender still has questions about making the loan, and your ability to document one or two things will eliminate them, the request for information can come prior to docs or prior to the creation of the final loan documents. If you face a request prior to funding, the lender has decided that you are a good bet, and is just "crossing the t's" to ensure that the deal is sound and salable to the secondary market. Requests made prior to closing are often conditions that might be waived, yet providing additional documentation dresses up your package.

 Any documentation you supply at any time in the loan approval process can lead to conditions that will complicate or abort the process.

Examples of prior to docs conditions include, but are not limited to, signing an IRS form 4506 to allow the lender to get a complete copy of your tax returns from the IRS.

 Be sure you specify on the 4506 which years of tax returns the lender may secure. Do not simply sign the form, giving the lender *carte blanche* to request an unlimited number of tax returns. Never alter any information on copies of your tax returns that you provide the lender. Not only is this a dishonest act, but it is one that will be detected if the lender gets copies of your returns directly from the IRS. There are people who have tried to do this to make their adjusted gross income (AGI) seem higher, but this is such an empty-headed tactic, they're not even popular with the other fraudulent inmates.

Another condition of funding required by the lender may be to provide an IRS form 9501 to verify AGI. The IRS can theoretically provide the information within hours of a request from a legitimate source. Normally, this request would come with a full doc loan, quick qualifier, or alt doc loan.

 A variation of more than 15 percent between your reported AGI and the figure shown on IRS 9501 will spark an in-depth review.

Self-employed people take note of the trap here. The Fannie Mae 1003 loan application requests your gross monthly income, not your AGI, on a quick qualifier. This is because the underwriter will look at your business-related liabilities as reported and deduct them from the gross income to arrive at your AGI. Your tax returns, however, will reflect your AGI, as calculated after you itemize your business expenses on your Schedule C. Discrepancies can easily arise if you are not meticulous and consistent about separating personal expenses from business expenses.

You are especially at risk if you use your personal charge card, or other personal accounts for business expenses. The underwriter is likely to count certain liabilities twice, because they are reported two different ways: one on your credit report, and one on your tax return. Provide six months of canceled business checks covering expenses to prove that an account is dedicated to business use.

At any point, the lender may require an inspection to confirm work completed according to the purchase contract. The lender will demand copies of all specific reports requested by a buyer on the purchase contract, such as a termite inspection. If an inspection yields a recommendation like "wood rot in kitchen needs to be repaired at an estimated cost of $3,000," the lender can require that the repair be made before moving forward. In such a circumstance a seller might require the buyer to make the earnest money deposit or part of it non-refundable to cover the cost of the work.

 When you get your purchase contract, you can check the boxes next to types of inspection you want. This alerts the lender to ask for the resulting written report. One alternative method of receiving inspections is verbally, which does not alert the lender, nor require an underwriter to get involved with your negotiating over the work on the house. However, any problems reported either in writing or verbally that relate to health and safety must be fixed before continuing through the Mortgage Maze!

 By specifying that a problem must be fixed, the lender puts the seller on formal notice. Even if you loan doesn't go through after that, it is the seller's obligation to disclose this condition to other buyers.

If you get your inspection report verbally, it is always your option to have that report put in writing at a price negotiated between you and the inspector.

During the loan process, the lender may ask the appraiser to justify any adjustments, upward or downward, from the *Fair Market Value* of the property. The appraiser's reason for an upward adjustment might be the view, location or quality of construction. A downward adjustment could be tied to functional obsolescence or lack of quality materials in the structure. Lenders routinely question appraisers because of the subject nature of their report even though they almost always insist that the appraiser be approved by them. For example, a view adjustment, might be $50,000 with one appraiser and $100,000 with another. It can go up or down depending on whether one man's view is seen as another man's lack of privacy. One of the contributing factors to the S&L crisis was that lending institutions didn't exercise consistent appraisal guidelines, so properties were often over-appraised.

Although the borrower cannot order an *appraisal* because it is an arms-length transaction initiated by the lender, the borrower is the one who usually pays for the report. Regardless of who pays, request a copy of the complete report.

The lender may ask for an explanation of easements on the subject property prior to funding. For example, an explanation why someone else might have a claim to air rights or why neighbors have the ability to drive across your property to enter their home. They also commonly accommodate the needs of utility companies. Because easements apply to someone else's use of a portion of your property, they go with the sale of the property, are rarely changeable, and prohibit you from building on them or otherwise impeding access.

TRUE STORY: FLOOD ZONE OR NOT

Seth and Martha Cohen's purchase of a condominium proceeded without a hitch until their lender made a prior to docs requirement for flood certification. Flood certifications started becoming a standard requirement after the massive mid-1990s floods in the Midwest. This came as a surprise to the Cohens since their real estate agent and appraiser said the property was not in a flood zone. The condo association's flood insurance policy also excluded their property, further evidence that it was not in a flood zone.

With reports in hand, the distraught Cohens went to their broker. After being challenged by the broker, the lender said that its independent insurance service had determined that the condo was in a flood zone. The broker secured a 40-page insurance binder showing exactly which properties were in the flood zone. The Cohen property was not among those in the zone. It is not uncommon for property, or even a portion of it, to be in a flood zone whereas the neighboring properties or remainder of the house are not.

Through the independent source, it was clear that all the neighboring properties were in a flood zone, and through a fluke, the Cohen property had been omitted from the records. Therefore, even though flood insurance had never been a condition of the loan because no one realized the property was in a flood zone, the lender's prior to docs research made it critical to approval.

Even though the additional insurance protected the borrowers, the Cohens had good reason to be upset with all the reporting agencies. The purchase closed a week late, with their furniture sitting in a moving truck the whole time at the cost of $125 per day. They also had to pay for motel accommodations. Their realtors picked up the added costs.

Flood maps change with the tides.

Prior-to-funding conditions could include a host of things, most of which fall into the umbrella category of passing quality control measures. These steps are normally taken after the loan has been approved and is headed for closing. It is the last set of things to be done to ensure that no major financial changes have occurred since the application was first processed.

LAST-MINUTE QUALITY CONTROL MEASURES

On the loan application the lender does a final check to ensure that all areas are complete, there are no changes to income, no liquid or tape cover-up masks original information, and the application is signed and dated by the borrower. The lender will cross-check signatures to be sure that the borrower's true signature is on all the documents. (As of January 1, 1996, all borrowers in the State of California also have to provide a thumbprint.)

The lender will reorder a current in-house credit report to ensure that you did not incur new debt since you first qualified. Inquiries, which point to your attempt to secure additional credit, will also spark a delay and investigation. At the close of escrow, your credit information will be updated and changes in your ratios made if deemed necessary by the lender. After signing your loan documents at escrow, the lender will do a final review of loan balances, as well as payoff demands of mortgage liens from lenders that are related to late payments of installment loans.

There is last-minute diligence regarding your income, too. If you are salaried and your pay documents are computerized, the lender will look to see that W2s and paystubs match (lenders request the most current pay stubs when the loan process has taken more than 30 days), and that verifications of employment (VOE) match W2s/paystubs. Detection of a pay increase wouldn't upset anyone, of course. The written VOE gives the lender a contact person to call for last-minute telephone verification of employment.

If you are salaried and your pay documents are not computerized, then three months of pay stubs should match three months of bank statements. You should also have 1040s and W2s handy to verify income, and the FICA (i.e., social security deduction) on the W2s and stubs must match current rates. Here again, there will be a final verification of your employment by calling your employer.

If you are self-employed, have three to six months bank statements on hand to verify income, just in case the lender has questions. You should also be prepared to avert last minute delays with two years' 1040s and year-to-date P&L and balance sheet, canceled checks to show payments match page 2 of your 1040, and your accountant's name and phone number. The lender may actually call your accountant to verify legitimacy and possibly check on that person's status as a registered tax preparer in good standing.

The lender might ask probing questions of your accountant, such as, how long you have been self-employed. There are two things to note here: 1) Your accountant has the right to ask the lender to put the request in writing, and many exercise it. 2) If you recently hired your accountant, you need to equip that person with copies of your records and/or tell the lender that the relationship is new.

Being self-employed could involve other paperwork as well. If your income records are on an IRS Form 1099 because you're a consultant, for example, see that the 1099s match the entry on Schedule C of the tax return. The lender will probably also check to ensure your income is consistent between tax returns and P&L, so that it is clear where your business-related finances end and your personal finances begin.

If you do a no income stated package, it's very important that your 1003 and RMCR contain no discrepancies, and that you can verify liquid assets of approximately six months. Remember that no IRS forms should be requested, because there is no stated income to verify.

If you do a quick qualifier, keep the above notes in mind, but know that IRS forms will be requested.

The status of your deposits could also provoke scrutiny or delays as you near the end of the Mortgage Maze. Be sure that verifications of deposit (VOD) were mailed directly to your lender and three months' bank statements are available to verify that no large deposits were made. Also, get ready to explain any deposit over the amount of your salary, because it's bound to look like a loan or undeclared gift to the lender.

As a preface to the next set of quality control issues, here is an explanation of the approaches to an appraisal, the method used to determine the value of a property. There are three approaches, two that relate to the property itself, and one that relates to the use of the dwelling. An owner-occupied dwelling will be appraised through a comparative market analysis and an evaluation of what the replacement cost of the home would be.

The first approach is a comparison of sales prices of similar properties recently sold in the area for the purpose of determining the fair market value of the property. These data are called the "comps."

The second approach assigns dollar value per square foot to various areas of the dwelling to arrive at a replacement cost. For example, because of where a property is and how it is built, an appraiser might assign a value of $100 per square foot to the interior living space. The adjoining two-car garage might be valued at $40 per square foot. The laundry room and fireplace might be $3,000, and the deck and patio areas might have a combined value of $20,000. In addition, the land itself would have a certain value. The appraiser would then calculate a reasonable depreciation on the property to complete the cost approach.

Finally, if a dwelling will not be owner-occupied, an addendum to the appraisal reflects a third approach. This involves a rental market survey to determine the property's income-generating potential. There is often an additional charge for this service.

Main quality-control issues tied to appraisals relate to over supply, the appearance of the property in the context of the neighborhood, additions, and comps that are over six months old, or that include properties that aren't in the neighborhood.

- "Over-supply" could cause a declining value in the property and likelihood of requiring more than six months' marketing, therefore making it ineligible for maximum LTV. A large number of comparable homes, perhaps all built by the same developer in a contained area within a short period of time, often creates a declining market. There is a high probability none of the properties in that development will appreciate for quite some time— normally until the project is completely sold out—so a lender would be unwilling to give maximum LTV.

- A property should conform to the area, that is, it does not "stick out" like a 5,000 square-foot home in a neighborhood populated by 1,500 square-foot homes. This kind of overbuilding, which might be the result of ambitious renovations, doesn't necessarily create a correspondingly higher property value. The owner might ask a lot more for it than other properties in the neighborhood are worth, but your attempt to convince a lender that the high price is warranted will meet with resistance.

- Additions must either be permitted or not included in square footage. The addition of a garage, for example, that was made without a permit from the jurisdiction excludes the square footage of the garage from the property specifications. The fair market value of the property wouldn't include the value of the garage, therefore. There are some exceptions to this. For example, the lender might concur that the modification brought the property into conformance with others in the area. (If everyone else in the neighborhood has a garage, you should have a garage, too.)

- Comps should be nearby and have sold within the previous six months, and there must be a good explanation if that's not the case. "Nearby" can mean different things, depending on where the property is located. Whereas a nearby rural property could be two miles away, a nearby city property would be two blocks away.

Also, in doing quality control checks, the lender will look for any seller credit that has not been reported as part of the purchase contract. Instead, it would be reported on the closing statement from the title company. The credit may arise if a contractor's report, for example, notes that there is a leak in the bathroom that is causing a weak floor, but the problem wasn't picked up by the appraiser because it was in an "inaccessible" area. If the borrower confronts the seller, the seller may decide to grant a credit of several thousand dollars. If the lender isn't aware of it until the final documents have been compiled, the lender might question the rate and terms of the loan. This is because the seller credit essentially changes the loan-to-value (LTV) ratio which influences rate and terms.

A credit from the seller can change the LTV of the loan to the extent that mortgage insurance becomes a condition of the loan. If, for example, you have put 20 percent down on the purchase of a house, and the seller gives you a credit equal to 4 percent that is not for non-recurring closing costs, it would lower your down payment to 16 percent. At this point, the lender would require you to get mortgage insurance (MI)—a policy paid for by the borrower with no benefit to the borrower. MI protects the lender from a higher perceived risk. Ultimately, the seller credit might not be such a great deal: Through mortgage insurance, your lender gets loss coverage of 15 to 25 percent and you don't even get a tax deduction.

Lenders love MI because it takes the risk away from them in case of default. Those lenders who tell you they don't charge MI invariably charge higher rates, margins and/or life cap, depending on the type of loan you select. The best way for you to deal with MI is to build the cost into your interest, not opt for a separate policy. By doing this, at least you get a tax deduction.

If any of the above quality control checks yields information that conflicts with or doesn't support claims that you have made in your documentation, the approval process is in jeopardy. And the information doesn't have to be negative for the lender to force a slow-down or temporary halt in the process, as the following story illustrates.

TRUE STORY: PRIVATE SAVINGS ACCOUNT JEOPARDIZES LOAN

In reviewing Bridgette Gilder's bank statements, the lender discovered that ATM transfers had been made to another account, one that she did not report on her application. To Bridgette, the account was her "private savings," used strictly for vacations and recreational equipment. Since she had no intention of applying the money to her house, she didn't think to mention the account, containing $6,000, in her 1003 loan application.

The presence of the money actually enhanced Bridgette's financial profile, but the omission of information about it delayed her final loan approval. Once the underwriter at the bank spotted the one discrepancy, he went looking for others.

WHY YOUR ROAD MIGHT HAVE A DETOUR

As hard as it might be, take a look at your situation from a lender's perspective. The lender is in business to make money and must be sure customers aren't lying. With these thoughts in mind, the lender develops a list of "red flags" and backup reviews to protect the investors from a bad business decision.

Courtesy of Fannie Mae, there is a comprehensive list of red flags in the loan package that alert an underwriter or broker to irregularities in data submitted by the borrower. These discrepancies do not condemn a person to rejection. Instead, they highlight the need for explanation. Following is a list of a few that may help you take control of your own situation and application in advance of a challenge.

RED FLAGS ON THE LOAN APPLICATION

Your current and proposed housing situations should make sense to a lender, and if your loan application reflects an odd circumstance, a red flag will go up. Consider these examples of flag-raising statements on the application:

- There are four dependents and only two bedrooms.

- The borrower lives with her parents. Lenders feel that it is unlikely that parents would provide a negative VOR, even if no rent was ever paid.

- A young borrower has a large accumulation of unsubstantiated assets.

- The borrower pays no rent at his current residence.

RED FLAGS ON THE VERIFICATION OF DEPOSIT (VOD)

There are numerous ways a simple VOD can complicate the loan process in its final stages. In short, if your account is new, large in relation to your income, or you don't have a bank account, the lender will investigate further.

Red flags also go up for these reasons:

- An IRA is shown as a liquid asset or a source of down payment. There is a substantial penalty, generally around 50 percent, for a premature withdrawal of an IRA. You can use an IRA as a source of down payment, but be careful not to record the full value of the IRA as your liquid asset.

- The bank account is not in the borrower's name. If your money is in an account named for your business, or in a trust fund, the lender must be sure how much access and control you have.

- The VOD contains an illegible bank employee signature with no further identification. Bank employees providing a VOD do not have the luxury of bad penmanship as doctors do. A lender will suspect forgery if a signature does not seem complete or at all readable.

- There is evidence of alterations or an ink eradicator, that is, "white out." The VOD must be clean, or the lender has every reason to suspect fraud.

RED FLAGS ON THE VERIFICATION OF EMPLOYMENT (VOE)

Since employment is such a critical factor in qualifying for a mortgage, lenders can get very picky about the VOE. Some of the most innocent errors, such as typing "July 4" instead of "July 3" as a hiring date, can raise a red flag. Believe it or not, an underwriter might even look at a perpetual calendar to determine if the hiring date you list is a weekend.

Another problem could be that your current and prior employment overlap. This can easily happen after a layoff, when a company technically keeps you on the payroll and provides benefits during a transition period, when you are actually free to accept employment with another company. Just explain it.

Appearances are important, too. If your employer uses a mail drop or post office box for conducting business, the lender assumes the business wants to "hide." And if your prior employer is no longer in business, be prepared to offer a reason why and to provide the name of a reputable source of information about your past employment.

RED FLAGS ON THE TAX RETURNS

Fundamentally, anything on your tax returns should match information provided on your loan application. That goes for addresses and occupation, as well as numbers.

Lenders also question why a high-bracket taxpayer would not use a professional tax preparer. It seems unfair to assume that just because you have money you want to hire someone else to look after it. Nevertheless, lenders assume it. This may change, however, as more and more savvy taxpayers manage their returns with software.

RED FLAGS ON THE W2 FORM

Sometimes, after submission of your records to a tax preparer, your accountant may send you a photocopy of the W2 for your personal file and it may not be of Copy C, the "Employee's Copy." It may inadvertently be Copy A (Federal return) or Copy B (State return). Check it, and tell your accountant that you want the original Copy C returned to you to avoid having a red flag go up when you submit W2s to a lender.

A lender would also question the legitimacy of a handwritten or typed W2. It's the computer age. Most companies don't do that anymore.

RED FLAGS ON THE CREDIT REPORT

Among the credit-related items that pique a lender's skepticism are a few that are bound to aggravate you. For example, a giant red flag goes up when a potential borrower has no credit record. It is so rare that an adult individual in the United States has no credit record, that the lender immediately suspects an alias has been used. You are also in for extra scrutiny if you are a high-income borrower with no "prestige" credit cards. It may sound discriminatory, but it is logical for a lender to suspect there is something amiss if you have means without taking advantage of major credit cards. People who eschew the use of credit cards, but have financial savvy, know that careful use and paying off the accounts each month is better than not having them.

Other problems include a variance in employment or residence date from other sources, recent inquiries from other mortgage lenders, and former place of business listed on the credit report, instead of the new one. Even if you are self-employed, your credit report should reflect that.

STORIES OF HORROR AND HAPPY ENDINGS

The following stories are probably the best method of illustrating how last-minute snags can force you to go a few extra miles to get through the Mortgage Maze.

TRUE STORY: TOO MUCH DILIGENCE LEADS TO DEAD END

Lena Miller's obsession with a particular property ultimately forced her to take a major detour in the Mortgage Maze. She lost the deal and had to backtrack to get another one.

The $550,000 condominium she wanted to buy had a deck suffering from wood rot and a floor damaged when a local utility company left its nearby work area uncovered during a major rainstorm. After the initial appraisal, she was stung by the lender's demands for repairs to the floor prior to the loan funding. She had hoped that the utility company's letter assuming full responsibility for the repair would suffice. Since it didn't, work on the floor commenced.

In a similar move, Lena's real estate agent concurrently suggested that Lena place a demand that the deck be repaired prior to final loan approval. Her concern stemmed from the fact that the pest inspector's report, which noted the wood rot, indicated that the adjacent wall could not be inspected since it was inaccessible. Only a complete inspection and follow-on repair of the deck would ensure the area was structurally sound. The seller of the condo made a reasonable offer to put $23,000, the estimated cost of repairs, into escrow so the deal could proceed. Lena rejected it, insisting the work be completed.

Six weeks after Lena received a conditional approval on her loan, all the work was done, and she was finally ready to move forward. The day of funding, scheduled for noon, the lender did a final quality-control check, a call to her office to verify employment. The call was made at 11:00; Lena had been fired at 9:00. Her six-month sojourn ended with a firm rejection.

From the seller's perspective, her good faith effort bought her a lot of frustration. Since all deposits were returned when the lender turned Lena down, the seller got nothing in the short term. She found out later she could have protected herself in other ways. Another appraisal, for example, might have yielded a different result. She also could have offered to put 150 percent of the estimated cost of the repairs in escrow, which might have allowed the escrow to close on a timely basis or firmly maintained there was no health or safety issue involved. If she'd made a concession on price and insisted that Lena "take it or leave it" as is, the deal would have gone through.

Funding is the day you and the lender put all the money in escrow. *Closing* is the day the transaction is recorded in the jurisdiction where the property is located.

A common case of naiveté, without negative implications, involves first-time home buyers trying to "pump up" their assets to look more attractive to a lender.

TRUE STORY: UNDERSTANDING AND MEETING LENDER DEMANDS

Joan and Robert Rubella married just after Joan began her law career and Robert entered his residency in orthopedics. Two years later, when they wanted to buy a $300,000 house, her salary was $65,000 and his was $72,000. When they went to a lender for a prequalification, they had $12,000 in savings, not even enough for a 5 percent down payment, and IRAs totaling $8,000. The loan officer winked and told them, "If you want a good loan, come back when you can put at least 10 percent down."

They went to their parents. One set of parents deposited $7,500 in their account; one deposited $10,000.

With hope in their hearts, Joan and Robert went to a broker, who helped them package their application. At first, everything looked good. Even their verification of deposit came back with the promising information that their declared assets matched their bank balance. In this instance, their bank was one of many that does not routinely provide a weighted average balance. The VOD simply reported Joan and Robert's current balance.

After giving conditional approval to the loan, the bank's underwriter requested two months' bank statements to ascertain the average balance. In a minute, she saw that two large deposits had been made 45 days prior to the conditional approval. Temporarily, the deal was off. Lenders need to know that your capacity to buy a house has a basis in continuing revenue streams.

This was just a quick detour for Joan and Robert. Once they understood that the lender would make the same loan if they could prove that at least 5 percent of the down payment came from them and the remainder from gifts, they took these steps:

1. Committed their savings of $12,000 to the down payment;

2. Cashed in their IRAs, which gave them roughly half the value, or $4,000, to add to the down payment (they knew they had 60 days to replace the money without penalty); and

3. Declared their parents' deposits as gifts and got the appropriate letters from them.

 There are two easy ways to by-pass the issue of a cash influx: 1) Transfer the funds more than 90 days in advance of initiating your loan process, and 2) if you are a co-signatory on your parent(s)' account, the funds would be considered seasoned, so the transfer of funds would not be an issue.

The short lesson in this discussion of detours is to make sure that your information about capacity, credit, collateral, and character is accurate and matches in all records. If there are discrepancies, explain them well rather than distort any record to create a match.

And now that you're past the delays, you can proceed to closing.

Chapter 9

Right Around the Corner: Manage the Closing

When you are getting close enough to your new home to smell the crackling fire, be excited, but also beware. The closing costs should be a fair representation of services rendered by mortgage professionals who are there to ensure that both the lender and the borrower are protected.

But you need to be aware of tasks and costs near the end of the Mortgage Maze that range from annoying to threatening.

You play a pivotal role in organizing those closing tasks and understanding which costs can be avoided or reduced, and which ones might change for good reasons. Only then can you move ahead to the closing with certainty about what the ultimate cost of the loan will be.

WHAT HAPPENS AT CLOSING?

In many parts of the country, there is a settlement or closing meeting involving the buyer and the seller, but in other places there is no meeting. Another scenario is that you or your authorized agent attends the meeting, but the person conducting it has the obligation to deliver the settlement statement to you as soon as possible after it. Since there really is no national standard to the closing process, what you experience may be a little different from what is described here. Nevertheless, the services and payments would be the same.

THE PARTICIPANTS

A representative of the title company or a lawyer serves as a third, neutral party in your transaction in its final stages. This is the individual who comes to the table with proof that public records indicate that the person who is selling the property owns the rights to it, and may transfer those rights to the buyer. Whether the third party is from a title company or is a practicing attorney depends on the state in which the transaction occurs. In any case, in most real estate transactions the buyer secures a *title insurance* policy to protect his or her claim to a valid title. A title insurance company determines insurability of the title during the search process, and will, at its own expense, defend the title and pay losses within the coverage of the policy if they occur.

When a lawyer serves as the third party, the culmination of the transaction is called a roundtable closing. In short, the buyer hands the seller the money, the seller hands the buyer a title, and the lawyer hands the buyer the legal documents on the title as other aspects of closing.

At closing, the third party takes instructions from all the Mortgage Maze participants. The list of additional players involved, but not necessarily present at a closing meeting other than in invoice-form, includes you, your agent (who might be an attorney or a broker), the seller, the seller's agent, the inspector(s), appraisers, property hazard-insurance agents, a representative of the lending institution, and a notary. They've all done this before, and they know what to expect. Nevertheless, a fabulous irony often surfaces: In this process, which is becoming more impersonal and automatic by the day, the participants in your closing meeting are likely to celebrate with you. Closing may be the most human moment in the Maze. It makes signing that stack of papers almost pleasant.

THE FINAL DOCUMENTS

From front to back, or top to bottom, you are likely to read and sign a large stack of documents ostensibly produced by the Department of Redundancy Department. Here are some of the possibilities.

Borrower's Escrow Instructions. The company conducting escrow business provides you with a breakdown of all the charges related to the transaction. On the credit side, you'll see the amount of money being loaned to you. On the debit side, you'll see the amount that you owe to the lender and to others who have provided mortgage-related services to you.

There is a balance on the credit and debit sides and those funds are required to match. On the credit side you will have the loan from the bank or seller and contributions, the deposit you gave at the time you wrote your original purchase contract, and your down payment and your closing costs which you bring to escrow. On the debit side, you have a seemingly endless list of charges that should have been disclosed to you along the way.

Lender's Instructions to Escrow Company. This is an outline of all the necessary documentation to be signed and notarized, then recorded at the county seat. Also included are any additional actions to be taken by the borrower or broker upon receipt of the above-mentioned documents. The lender's quality-control inspection of the package yields the complete list of items. If everything is correctly executed, the lender will fund the loan the day before closing.

Your and the seller's instructions to the escrow company were in your purchase agreement.

Grant Deed. This states that title to the property is moving from one person(s) to another.

Change of Ownership Report. Your jurisdiction requires this form upon the transfer of real property. It gives the people who send you tax bills and official notices a record of the transfer. You might view it as an occasion to boost the taxes based on your purchase price.

Fixed (or Adjustable) Rate Note. A Fixed Rate Note is a simple, straightforward document with your interest rate. If you have an ARM, you will see an Adjustable Rate Note that explains to you how your rates are calculated, when they take effect, what your life cap is, and so on.

Deed of Trust. The Deed of Trust is six pages of notes telling you that you'd better pay as agreed, maintain your property and insurance, and don't step outside of your agreement with the lender in any other way, or else the lender will do various horrible things to your credit and sanity.

Riders. If you have an ARM, you would have an *Adjustable Rate Rider* detailing the terms of your loan. You might also have a 1–4 Family Rider, which holds you to using the property as you said you would, not turning it into a multi-unit apartment building, for example.

Truth-in-Lending Disclosure. The full title of this document should the "final, final truth-in-lending disclosure" since it follows other truth-in-lending disclosures made earlier in your loan process. It tells exactly what you are supposed to pay and to whom, including how much in interest you will pay over the life of the loan. In accordance with the Real Estate Settlement Procedures Act (*RESPA*) of 1973, the lender and other professionals providing a mortgage-related service to you are required to give you truth-in-lending disclosures upfront. This is so you have a reasonable idea, every step of the way, of what your ultimate costs will be. Since you may request additional services or you may decide to go from a fixed rate to an adjustable one, for example, the total amount you owe could easily change. The truth-in-lending disclosure provided as part of your closing package is the last word.

Itemization of Amount Financed. This is yet another statement of what you pay to whom for what.

Occupancy Affidavit and Financial Status. This is your statement that your owner-occupied property is owner occupied, or will be within 30–60 days of the close of escrow, depending on the lender. Your pledge is also to occupy that property as your principal residence for at least a year, a condition you will also see in the Deed of Trust. It also makes you promise, once again, that there have been no material changes in your financial status.

Signature Affadavit. People with bad penmanship take note. This document is a notarized copy of your legal signature. Your chicken-scratch on all your loan documents better be a good match for what appears here.

Flood Insurance Authorization. Even if you are not in a flood zone now, this document makes you promise if your property ever becomes part of a flood zone, you will get the appropriate insurance.

Notice of Right to Cancel. This is for owner-occupied residences and it is powerful. It is an absolute right to cancel the entire deal, without penalty, within three business days "from whichever of the following events occurs last: 1) Transaction Date (date you sign loan documents), or 2) The date you received your Truth in Lending disclosures, or 3) The date you received this notice of your right to cancel."

All you have to do is give your lender notice within that time frame, not including Sundays or national holidays, that you want out, and you are out. The proper way to do it is to cancel by mail or telegram, although you could personally deliver the notice. Verbal notice has also withstood the test in some cases, but it should always be followed up with written notice.

This "right of rescission" is another consumer protection related to the law called RESPA, although use by a consumer can lead to disappointment as much as it can to relief. Here are two stories that illustrate the contrast.

TRUE STORY: PULLING OUT COSTS MONEY

After a television broadcast highlighted dropping interest rates, Julia and Johnnie Dealer called their escrow officer and told him that the deal they had signed a day before was off. They knew their rights, and thought they could save thousands over the life of their loan by waiting a week or two and restructuring the deal. Three days later, they realized their action had been hasty and called the escrow officer to retract their statement. By that time, he had dutifully notified the lender, and the entire package essentially went into the shredder.

Julia and Johnnie maintained that their verbal cancellation wasn't legal; they wanted their deal back. The lender countered, "I respected the fact that you exercised your rights in the given time and acted accordingly."

The lender then offered them precisely the same loan, which they accepted, and charged them a fee to redraw the documents.

There is a special reason why this next story is about a vacuum cleaner, not a house. It highlights one of the key reasons that "right of rescission" legislation came into being: high-pressure, door-to-door sales.

TRUE STORY: SUCKED IN BY THE VACUUM

Eddie Grover came home one Friday afternoon from a week-long business trip. Greeting him, alongside his smiling wife, was a $1,600 vacuum cleaner. His wife, April, touted its virtues as demonstrated to her by the kindly lady who came to the door and sold it to her two days before. April was even proud of the hard bargain she drove: She traded in her new $300 vacuum cleaner with the company for a whopping $525 credit, thereby reducing the cost of the new one to only $1,075. Eddie's call to the office listed on the contract got him a ringing phone—not even voice mail.

Not only was Eddie unimpressed, he was livid. He called a friend in the real estate business who had recently explained rights of rescission to him and asked, "Does this apply to vacuum cleaners?" It did, and he promptly went to the post office and mailed a registered letter to the company that called off the deal. He also happened to enclose his business card, which read, "Edward Grover, County Sheriff."

Monday morning he got an apologetic call from the vacuum cleaner company, as well as the opportunity to buy one for the showroom price of $800 with no trade-in required. He declined.

Impound Authorization and First Payment Notification. As the name implies, an impound is money that is "locked up." This document says you understand that the lender is going to lock up a certain amount of your money in escrow to have funds available to pay property taxes and insurance premiums for the property.

For example, you may be required to pay 14 months' worth of hazard insurance in advance. This ensures that you have a year of the insurance paid in-full, and a two-month credit. If your hazard insurance goes up 10 percent the next year, that two-month credit is applied to the increase, and the amount of your next 12 months of payment is adjusted upward by 10 percent. Again, this gives the lender the comfort of knowing that there will still be reserves in your account if the premium escalates the following year, and so on for the life of the loan.

It has happened that a lender inadvertently or deliberately required an overly large sum in escrow. The necessary adjustments to the borrowers' accounts came swiftly after a class-action suit.

There is an impound schedule for taxes that is based on requirements of the jurisdiction. In many locations, borrowers can remember their property tax payment schedule with the phrase "No darn fooling around!"—a memory trigger for November 1 (semi-annual taxes are due), December 10 (taxes must be paid by then, or they're late), February 1 (taxes are due), April 10 (they're late).

Name Affadavit (AKA). This applies to people who have had a name change, such as a person recently married who adopted the name of the spouse, and other borrowers with AKAs on their credit report.

Compliance Agreement. In this brief statement, you promise to cooperate with the lender in adjusting for clerical errors and other little mistakes that put the loan documents out of compliance. It also includes items that are needed, but were somehow missed.

Borrower's Certification and Authorization Letter. It's one more piece of paper that says your lender can verify what you've said, that you didn't misrepresent your status, and so on.

Notice to Applicant of Right to Receive Copy of Appraisal Reports. It used to be that lenders would charge an application fee and not charge you an appraisal fee. It got them off the hook from providing you with a copy. Now, most lenders charge you the appraisal fee and offer you a copy of the report. This document alerts you that it's yours for the asking.

Audit Authorization. If asked for this, you acknowledge that you have provided tax returns as part of your loan package and that the lender will audit within a certain period after closing.

Quality Control Announcement and Authorization. This advises you that your loan might be part of a random audit loan-selection process, sparked by investor request.

IRS Form 4506. Here's the warning on this one again: The 4506 gives your lender the right to request your tax returns from the IRS, so be sure to specify in block 10 the tax period(s) you are allowing the lender to review. Remember, this form should not be included if you are doing a no-income stated package. This caveat applies to the next form as well.

Request for Validation of Income (IRS Form 9501).

Servicing Disclosure Statement. This covers the fact that servicing of your loan may be transferred by your lender to another institution. It also reminds you of your consumer rights regarding the servicing of your loan.

Get your pen ready to sign those docs and write those checks!

THE NATURE OF CLOSING COSTS

As a borrower, you don't necessarily have to pay all closing costs. Sometimes, it is possible to make a deal with the seller to cover those one-time items called non-recurring closing costs. These charges include the title examination, document preparation, appraisal, credit report, points, and lender fees. In other cases, the lender may have a policy of paying the appraisal fee.

Non-recurring closing costs (NRCCs) are a concession to you when paid by the seller. This is allowed by all lenders within limits that do not affect the LTV. See the caution in Chapter 8 about a seller credit for items other than NRCCs impacting your LTV.

Following are the LTVs with normal corresponding allowable maximum seller credit, based on the lesser of the sales price or appraised value in each case:

Regardless of the LTV, if the mortgage is fixed rate and the property is an investment property.	2 percent
If the LTV is greater than 90 percent and the property will be occupied as a principal residence.	3 percent
Same condition, if less than 90 percent LTV.	6 percent
If 80 percent LTV (or the combined LTV is 90 percent or less) and the property will be occupied as a second home.	6 percent

Your ability to negotiate with the seller over his or her contribution to NRCCs can create an important opportunity to save money in the long run, as well as at closing. In your purchase contract, there is an allowable limit stated on how much you can accept from the seller for NRCCs. In short, you can't take more than the actual NRCCs without affecting the LTV.

Let's say that the actual amount is $7,000, but your seller has already agreed to contribute as much as $10,000. First of all, congratulations on driving toward a better deal. Secondly, since you will not be allowed to leave money on the table after closing, use the additional money to increase your NRCCs by increasing the points paid. A point is 1 percent of the loan amount and additional money paid up front in points reduces your interest rate on the loan, therefore, your monthly payments.

NECESSARY TOLLS

The following screen image illustrates how reasonable non-recurring closing costs might stack up.

```
┌─ESTIMATED CLOSING COSTS ──────────────┐
│                                        │
│  Loan Origination Fee      2.00%   $1,600 │
│  Appraisal Fee                      $400 │
│  Credit Report                       $85 │
│  Tax Related Service Fee             $85 │
│  Processing Fee                     $250 │
│  Escrow/Closing Fee                 $280 │
│  Courier / Flood Report              $65 │
│  Title Insurance                    $225 │
│  Recording Fee                       $30 │
│  Miscellaneous Costs                $265 │
│  Total Closing Costs             $3,285 │
└────────────────────────────────────────┘
```

Rather than send you flipping through the glossary, here is an explanation of the costs listed on the screen and a sense of what is reasonable and what is normally out of line. Beware. There are those who will attempt to prey on you at closing because they are aware of your desire to complete the deal. For example, mortgage brokers and bankers may hit you with courier and wire fees that are unjustified.

Their hope is that "$20 here and $20 there" won't provoke a fight from you. Prove them wrong!

The lender charges an application fee to cover the lending institution's processing costs. The $350 listed here is average. With all the artificial intelligence involved with processing, this fee should be going down, not up.

The appraisal fee, which is sometimes paid by the lender, covers the services of a professional appraiser selected by the lender, or by the broker from the lender's approved appraiser's list. Remember that there are three approaches to appraisals, but if your property will be owner-occupied, the appraiser will use only two, namely, the replacement cost and comparable market data methods.

The attorney's fee will be payable if required by your state. Attorney's fees should not be astronomical for a normal real estate transaction. In its "Settlement Costs" guide, the U.S. Housing and Urban Development Department warns, "The U.S. Supreme Court has said that it is illegal for bar associations to fix minimum fee schedules for attorneys, so do not be bashful about discussing and shopping for legal fees you can afford."

As you saw in Chapter 3, it is possible for you to get a copy of your credit reports for free from the three main reporting agencies. Or you can get a consolidated report including your credit score from www.maze.com for about $30. Nevertheless, the lender's request for the consolidated and scored report, or RMCR, will cost a little over $50 and includes the cost of the last-minute copy or HUP. If it's much more, you should challenge the fee.

Credit and appraisal fees are normally paid up front, as are exact fees for services rendered.

The title company charges a title examination fee to perform a search to determine who has legal rights to the property. There have been cases where the seller had as much right to complete a transaction on a property as a squatter with a set of keys to the house. The title search is an important protection for you and the lender.

Even when a title search is performed, most lenders require title insurance as back-up protection that the seller-of-record has title to the property and can convey it freely and clearly without any known exceptions. *Title insurance* companies routinely issue two types of policies, the owner's, which covers you, and the lender's. The one-time fee varies, but it should be a matter of hundreds, not thousands, of dollars. Once a title policy is issued, if any claim covered under the policy is ever filed against your property, the title company will pay any legal fees involved in your (and their) defense, as well as covered losses relating to a valid claim.

You have the option of requesting several different kinds of home inspections, with some inspections leading to others when problems are found. The home inspection fees can add up but are highly recommended. A fee of $400 might cover pest and basic structural inspections.

You need to know as much as possible about every inch of your property. If you have ever been surprised by swarmers, which are termites with wings serving as "point men" for their troops, you know how traumatic it is being out of touch with the realities of your home. Paying for thorough inspections is money well spent.

When property changes hands, the jurisdiction charges transfer taxes. The seller pays a prorated tax to the date of transfer, or closing. You are responsible for all taxes related to the property after that.

A tax service fee goes to an outside service that checks to be sure that taxes on the property are current. Most property tax liens go before the first mortgage; you want to be absolutely certain liens are not present to impinge on your deal.

Document preparation is a bit of a catchall that won't necessarily be charged. Many lenders and escrow agents do assess it, however, for drawing up closing docs such as mortgage notes and deeds. Also called doc drawing fees, they are just another way for the lender and escrow agent to cover overhead.

Broker's Processing Fees are charged by most brokerages to cover their overhead, but most only charge a fee if that transaction is completed.

Thieves and Beggars on the Highway

Now that you've had a glimpse of legitimate closing costs, you are equipped to guard against the garbage fees. Garbage fees can include overnight delivery services, such as Federal Express, UPS, and Airborne that may or may not have been used, and courier services rendering door-to-door delivery. Use caution in reviewing overnight delivery and courier fees, don't assume they are ill-founded. If your payment is sent using such a service, it is possible that the speed resulted in interest savings for you.

Your husband stopped at the broker's office a couple times to pick up documents on his way home from work. You see a "courier service" fee of $50 on your settlement worksheet. Your broker says, "We hand-delivered these documents to you." What do you say? It's garbage, of course!

Underwriters are like appraisers and inspectors in the sense that they get paid regardless of whether or not your loan goes through. An underwriting review fee is not unreasonable by nature, but it is probably a garbage fee when charged by a mortgage broker in addition to the broker's commission.

Some document fees are garbage fees. Just be sure to ask exactly what service a document fee covers before you pay the extra $100 or $200.

Chapter 10

The Virtual Mortgage Maze: A Digital Drive-Through

By the time you navigate this Mortgage Maze or the next one, you will be confronted by a mortgage qualification process that includes more automated scoring systems, appraisal databases, and computerized reviews and standards. This databank of artificial intelligence will continue to play a larger role in borrower qualification.

If you are an easy A loan borrower, you will enjoy the quick turnaround which digital mortgages provide. If you are anything less than an A, the work you will do to comply with the conventional profiles will increase. Understanding how your financial information will be scrutinized and screened will help you navigate the digital Mortgage Maze.

THE DESKTOP MAZE

You have been introduced to the way computers aid financial data storage, reporting, and analysis. Add "decision making" to that list of duties, and you can see how the world of mortgage lending is moving toward artificial intelligence in its truest sense.

From a consumer's point of view, this isn't necessarily bad. Since the complexity of the mortgage application process—and its related costs—along with the cash required at settlement are the biggest barriers to homeownership for most people, streamlining the process through automation will be a vast improvement. There is no doubt it will reduce the anxiety level for the majority of prospective borrowers. Theoretically it can cut materials and administrative costs for lenders by reducing paperwork and processing time, and thereby reduce fees. It could make housing discrimination a thing of the distant past and offer specific advice on how to qualify for a specific loan product. On the other hand, computerized systems don't yet have the ability to consider compensating factors, like a consistent pattern of savings.

Another consumer advantage emerges from the impact that automated systems have on who originates loans. When the process is dominated by paper and multiple contributors to processing and analysis, the process is naturally dominated by big lenders, they either expedite or retard your progress through the maze. Computerization empowers smaller lenders and third-party originators to compete effectively with big institutions by using the same tools for underwriting, origination, and all aspects of the loan approval process. In a real sense this means more competition for your business and therefore the likelihood of a better deal.

A third advantage is the preservation of forests. As digital tools turn documents into bytes, the loan process requires less paper. When the average loan package contains 75 to 100 pages, with two copies prepared for the lender and one retained by the broker, mortgage transactions have traditionally meant the death of a lot of trees.

A fundamental concept in the automation of the mortgage process is electronic data interchange (EDI), which refers to the technical protocols that enable everybody in the financial chain to transmit information to each other. Whether the user relies on regular phone lines, fiber optic cable, or other transmission options doesn't matter. EDI reflects rules for document formatting and security that allow for consistent transmissions and internationally recognized standards for these protocols.

Using Freddie Mac's Prospector® and Fannie Mae's MORNET® as prime examples, here is a look at approaches to digitizing mortgage lending in the late-1990s, and where it is headed at the speed of light.

FREDDIE MAC'S PROSPECTOR®

Lending institutions are installing the software and connections for using Freddie Mac's Prospector, as are certain mortgage brokers who are approved by Freddie Mac and sponsored by a lender. At this stage of design, Prospector includes 25 fields of information tied to the loan application and yields an instant approval, denial, or referral to an underwriter for analyzing information provided by the borrower.

A complementary program enabling automated appraisals is available to the same professionals. If the subject property or a comparable property has been appraised through Freddie Mac before, and the information was entered into Freddie's database, an appraisal can reportedly be produced within 15 minutes, and the judgment from Prospector rendered with a package immediately ready for funding—just like that.

There is so much faith in this system that the mortgage originator who takes a Prospector-approved package to a sponsoring lender knows that the loan will go through. Freddie Mac's almighty computer has declared unconditionally that it's a done deal, so the lender has no need for explanations, verifications, statements, returns, or anything else except signatures on the loan documents. The originator can then draw up the loan docs and deliver them to title. The loan package can be signed and returned to the lender with the hard copy of the package.

Sound too good to be true? In a big way, it is. At this stage, Freddie Mac's computerized appraisal services, which are an integral part of the no-resistance package, apply only to a limited number of homes. Usually, these properties are part of a development, planned community, or complex where specifications on the subject properties have been entered into Freddie Mac's appraisal database. Prospector can still give a reading on the capacity and credit of a potential borrower, but often vital information on the collateral is missing. Therefore, the loan process may be expedited through Prospector, but it will not be lightening fast without the automated appraisal. Furthermore, the automated appraisal will lack adjustments from the subjective valuation of views, location, and so on.

Fannie Mae's MORNET®

Fannie Mae, like Freddie Mac, has an expressed commitment to using technology to lower mortgage-related costs, as well as risk to the lender. In March 1995, the company launched Fannie Mae's Financial Networks, self-described as "a family of open, flexible, and sophisticated systems we developed working with our customers to reduce costs and streamline activities throughout the mortgage cycle." Fannie Mae calls its primary program MORNET EDI.

The MORNET EDI system attempts to eliminate the multiple transmissions of documents to lenders. Like Prospector, it is designed to give lenders one source of nationwide mortgage origination and closing services. Fannie Mae goes one step further, however, with its Third Part Originator System (TPOS), which opens the door for more small companies to compete with big lending institutions in the mortgage origination field.

In addition, a triad of programs through an offshoot of MORNET called MORNETPlus™ is specifically for non-lenders. These Microsoft Windows-based offerings have the somewhat self-explanatory titles of Desktop Underwriter™, Desktop Originator™, and Desktop Home Counselor™. As with Prospector, mortgage brokers who use them must be a lender-sponsored participant. Following are Fannie Mae's own explanations of what they offer and what they promise:

Desktop Underwriter. This program analyzes a loan as if it were being handled by an underwriter. It may be used as a stand-alone system or integrated with other systems such as the Desktop Originator or other origination software. According to Fannie Mae's literature, it has the potential to speed up the approval process "enabling the underwriter to spend more time on more difficult loan applications." The premise is that "problem-free loans" (if there is such a thing) will fly through the process through rapid-fire online transactions.

This system does not have the ability to reject a loan application. This intent does seem to differentiate it from a product such as Prospector, by introducing the human rule: It takes one person to approve, and two to decline.

Desktop Originator. This program lets lenders equip originators with loan product and rate information so the originators can take applications, perform borrower analyses, and communicate with their lenders electronically. It allows lenders to build electronic loan files and provides the network capabilities to transmit them.

Desktop Home Counselor. Desktop Home Counselor is designed as an educational resource that aids lenders and nonprofit counselors in providing personal and financial information for low- and moderate-income borrowers, including credit and affordability analyses. A strong loan package should be able to move through the entire Fannie Mae or Freddie Mac automated process in one to two hours. Using Fannie Mae's tools in this example, here is how an alternative docs or limited docs loan could move so quickly.

The borrower would bring these documents to a mortgage broker: most recent 3-months' bank statements, W2s for past 2 years, paystubs for the most recent 30-day period, mortgage payment record, and the employer's telephone number.

The broker uses Third Part Originator System (TPOS) on the computer to prequalify, complete the application with necessary disclosures and other forms, and generate a transmittal form to go with the file. The broker then uses Desktop Originator to compare interest rates and loan products, pull a credit report, do a rate lock, and submit the file to a lender.

The lender uses Desktop Originator to receive and verify the case file. Then the lender uses Desktop Underwriter to secure an automated underwriting recommendation. The lender switches back to Desktop Originator to receive and confirm the rate lock and then transmits the decision and underwriting findings to the broker.

Using Desktop Originator, the broker reviews the status of the package and tells the borrower whether the package is approved, referred, or denied. In the near future, this process could take as little as thirty minutes or an hour. The only time left to add is the day(s) it takes for people to review county records to insure a free, clear, and transferable title.

AUTOMATED APPRAISALS

Just as the protocols for EDI of information on capacity and credit ensure that all parties handle it the same way, the same is true for automated appraisals. The preliminary standard format was called CAFE (Common Appraisal Format for Exchange), but it is being refined and reviewed for adaptation as an American National Standard for the industry.

Whereas other documents in the case file contain primarily text and rows of numbers, appraisals usually include photos, maps and sketches that may even contain annotations. Using whatever software allows the appraiser to adhere to the protocols, he or she can transmit all that information to one or several locations in minutes. The package would also include an electronic signature of the appraiser. Preliminary title reports and photos of all comps and subject property could be appended. In the future, satellite photos of the area and property could also be routine components.

As the appraisers themselves, as well as lenders, mortgage brokers, Fannie Mae, Freddie Mac, and others in the mortgage loop build archives of these electronically transmitted appraisals, the loan approval process can move at warp speed. Storage of the combined text/picture files can be stored on and readily accessed from CD-ROMs. How some of the critical subjective components of appraisals will be handled, however, remains to be seen.

This could bring up a concern for you that an "old" appraisal could be pulled out of the database and undermine your case on collateral. One thing is certain, appraisers aren't going to throw up their hands abruptly and say, "No one needs me any more. I'll go find something else to do." They will still be around to physically render services and help you feed a current appraisal into the automated system. And, as you will see in the discussion on multimedia, your own ability to supplement an appraisal is also sitting on top of your desk.

INTERNET MORTGAGES

All of the above-mentioned systems of information exchange rely on private networks which have security measures imbedded in them to protect your privacy and the information of all members of the network. It isn't as easy to do that on the World Wide Web.

While in the mid-1990s, much of the process can safely be completed over the Net, there is still personal financial data and most elements of closing that don't belong on an open network.

Fortunately, many Internet-based businesses are breaking ground in the area of electronic commerce and they have security measures in place that offer immediate hope for "Internet mortgages."

For example, a number of companies provide extensive, copyrighted text and graphics to professional researchers and newspapers over the Net. They do it through a system of account codes and have "firewalls" built into their software that make it very difficult, but it's never impossible, for non-subscribers to access the information. The proliferation of these kinds of services that deal with legally protected information will give rise to new, as well as more secure, approaches to data transfer over the Net.

Even more than complete mortgage services, what the Internet offers you right now is the ability to compare rates, download amortization schedules that reflect a situation you describe, input hypothetical information to review your options under different conditions, and get free advice through the Frequently Asked Questions and e-mail options at various sites such as www.maze.com and others listed in Appendix A. And you can do it all over a regular phone line.

THE MULTIMEDIA MORTGAGE MAZE

Concurrent with the use of technology to create a more automatic, non-human, loan process, its use can also bring borrowers and mortgage professionals closer together. The same computers that spit out approvals and rejections in blasts of 1s and 0s also allow for transmission of the sight and sound of a human.

In conjunction with their other desktop paraphernalia, real estate brokers, mortgage brokers, lenders, and others are using the multimedia capability of their computers for video-conferencing. Some also send audio clips with personal instructions to each other, as demonstrated at www.maze.com. The inhibitor is that video and audio material requires more bandwidth, or transmission capacity, than text files to be received in real time. Regular phone lines alone —the so-called "twisted pairs" of copper wire that are the dominant carrier in the U.S.—aren't yet up to the job.

Unless you and everyone around you has already moved completely into the digital age, this scenario is part of your future. You've investigated rates and done a self-qualification using software you downloaded from the Internet. With a fairly good idea of what you want and what you can get, you e-mail a mortgage broker and ask for a first meeting via video-conference. From that moment through to the closing video-meeting, when your broker, loan officer, escrow company representative, *et al.*, participate from their offices using their desktop video-conferencing capabilities, you have electronically managed your mortgage process. The process may have become an interactive multimedia experience, with you getting an e-mail or an audio file requesting an explanation of a credit problem, for example, and you instantly responding by return e-mail.

In using technology this way, you can see how the role of real live agents, loan officers, and mortgage brokers will also become more personal, not less personal. More than half the people who apply for home loans have financial profiles that are not conventional or easy for a computer to review. Their applications will most likely be labeled "refer," rather than "approve" or "deny." Many of these people will want counsel from professionals who know how to bring their package into conformance for automated review.

As an adjunct to these human helpers, you might also have access to "virtual agents." If your loan package is weak in a particular area, for example, an initial computerized review of your file would detect that and automatically create a digital helper for your case. The virtual agent would flag your trouble spots then produce the guidance and answers you need to get a speedy loan approval.

No matter how computerized the Mortgage Maze becomes, though, human beings will always find a way to keep themselves involved. And, as long as people are there, somebody will help you get around the winding turns and past the detours until you make it through.

The Maze Master's Glossary of Mortgage Terms

Definitions marked with * are excerpted from Student Study Guide for Real Estate Principles, Dennis J. McKenzie.

acceptable debt	Debt measured by this magic formula: For every dollar of debt, you need about three dollars of income to qualify for a mortgage.
adjustable rate mortgage (ARM)	Involves a low start rate with provisions for interest rate increases and decreases within predetermined adjustment and life caps; normally easier to qualify for than a fixed-rate mortgage.
adjustable rate rider	Details the complete terms of an adjustable-rate loan in the documents signed at settlement.
air rights	Ownership of everything upward from the property boundaries to space. Generally speaking, air rights contain an easement to accommodate flying aircraft.
ALTA	American Land Title Association
ALTA Owner's Policy*	An owner's extended coverage policy that provides buyers or owners the same protection the ALTA policy gives to lenders.
ALTA Title Policy*	A type of insurance policy issued by title insurance companies that expands the

risks normally insured against under the standard type policy to include unrecorded mechanic's liens; unrecorded physical easements; facts a physical survey would show; water and mineral rights; and rights of parties in possession, such as tenants and buyers under unrecorded instruments.

amortization

A repayment method in which the amount borrowed is repaid through regular monthly payments of principal and interest over a specific period of time.

annual percentage rate (APR)

The yearly interest percentage of a loan, as expressed by the actual rate of interest paid.

appraisal*

An estimate and opinion of value; a conclusion resulting from the analysis of facts.

appreciation

An increase in the value of the property in relation to a specific purchase price or point in time.

artificial intelligence

A computerized, deductive, analytical approach to decision making increasingly used by creditors to approve or deny a credit request. It is based on specific formulas relating to capacity, number of credit report inquiries, ratio of cash reserves to debt, amount of proposed down payment, and any other computerized information important to the lender.

assumption of mortgage*

The taking of title to property by a grantee, wherein he assumes liability for payment of an existing note secured by a mortgage or deed of trust against the property; becoming a co-guarantor for the payment of a mortgage or deed of trust note.

balloon note	A low-rate loan with payments insufficient to fully pay off or amortize the loan prior to its due date, so it moves to a dead-end situation. That is, you must pay off the remaining principal sum—or, make a balloon payment—at maturity.
bankruptcy	A legal recourse in the face of insurmountable debt.
bankruptcy scoring	Begins with a low score, then add points for bad behavior in an effort to predict the likelihood of your declaring bankruptcy—an inversion of the approach to credit scoring. This is a method of predicting your chance of going bankrupt.
bottom ratio	The percentage of your gross monthly income that the lender will allow for monthly housing costs plus all of your other monthly debt.
CC and Rs*	Abbreviation for covenants, conditions and restrictions.
capacity	Your ability to handle debt; one of the more objective criteria in determining borrowing power.
cash reserves	Money left over after down payment and closing costs are paid; a lender usually wants you to have at least two to three months of your total monthly payments in cash reserves.
character	The most subjective criteria used to determine your borrowing power; could be affected by how steadily you have been employed in the same field or how many years of school you've completed.

charge off	The term meaning your creditor gave up on you and closed the account without receiving the balance due. The creditor wrote off the account as uncollectable.
cleared monthly account (CLR)	An account that must be paid in full upon receipt of each statement. A type of account that appears on your credit report.
closing	The day the real estate transaction is recorded in the jurisdiction where the property is located.
closing costs	Fees and charges paid at the end of a real estate transaction.
closing statement*	An accounting of funds made to the buyer and seller separately. Required by law to be made at the completion of every real estate transaction.
collateral	One criterion used to determine your borrowing status; it relates to the property you are buying. Key considerations are price, condition and location of the subject property. The lender looks at resellability of the property in the event you default on the loan.
collection account (coll act)	Your creditor gave up on you and made you someone else's problem, that is, a collection agent.
collection item	A bill that has gone to a collection agent.
Community Reinvestment Act (CRA)	A law designed to ensure that low-income communities have a fair opportunity to borrow money from the banks that operate in their community.

compensating factors	Positive factors like perfect credit or greater than normal savings that can convince a lender to make certain concessions if other parts of the picture, like the qualifying ratios, are outside the limits.
condominium (condo)*	A system of individual fee ownership of units in a multifamily structure, combined with joint ownership of common areas of the structure and the land.
conforming loan	A loan no greater than $207,000.
construction loan*	Loan made for the construction of homes or commercial buildings. Usually funds are disbursed to the contractor-builder during construction and after periodic inspections. Disbursements are based on an agreement between borrower and lender.
conventional mortgage*	A mortgage securing a loan made by investors without governmental underwriting, that is, not FHA-insured or VA-guaranteed.
cost approach*	One of three methods in the appraisal process. An analysis in which a value estimate of a property is derived by estimating the replacement cost of the improvements, deducting therefrom the estimated accrued depreciation, then adding the market value of the land.
cost of funds	The cost of money for the savings and loan associations in a given area. For example, the 11th District Cost of Funds Index (COFI) is based on the cost of funds for a certain group of Western states.

credit	A criterion used to determine your borrowing power; it relates to your history of making payments on your obligations as agreed.
credit information service	*See* credit scoring.
credit scoring (credit information service)	A system of assigning a score to your record that is used by the credit reporting agencies. It reflects multiple factors, including the mix of revolving and installment credit, use of available credit, number of inquiries about your credit made recently, and more.
date of last delinquency (DLD)	Historical delinquency information on your credit report that indicates the last time—and it could be years ago—that you made a late payment.
debt-to-income ratio	The relationship of debt-to-income that lenders review to make an initial assessment of your capacity to handle debt over a prolonged period of time.
deed in lieu of foreclosure	An agreement between the lender and the borrower to return the property for full credit to the debt owed with minimal consequences and without foreclosure.
demand for pay-off	If you are refinancing, a demand for pay-off is requested by the title company to ascertain the exact amount you owe on your property. It would reflect your current lender's balance, daily interest and any late fees owed.
depreciation	A decrease in the value of the property from the time of purchase.
disposable income*	The after-tax income a household receives to spend on personal consumption.

down payment
: The amount of money you put toward the purchase price of the house; it determines your loan-to-value ratio.

earnest money
: An amount that you give upfront when you commit to buying a property. It shows you mean business.

equity*
: The interest or value that an owner has in real estate over and above the liens against it; branch of remedial justice by and through which relief is afforded to suitors in courts of equity.

escrow*
: The deposit of instruments and funds with instructions to a third neutral party to carry out the provisions of an agreement or contract; when everything is deposited to enable carrying out the instructions, it is called a complete or perfect escrow.

fair market value*
: This is the amount of money that would be paid for a property offered on the open market for a reasonable period of time with both buyer and seller knowing all the uses to which the property could be put and with neither party being under pressure to buy or sell.

Fannie Mae (Federal National Mortgage Association)
: Federally chartered but shareholder owned, it has a mission to provide products and services that make it more affordable for Americans to own homes; a quasi-governmental agency. It does this through the secondary mortgage market by buying mortgages from banks to replenish their cash for more mortgages.

Federal Deposit Insurance Corporation (FDIC)
: A federal agency that oversees banks.

Federal Home Loan Mortgage Corporation	*See* Freddie Mac.
Federal Housing Administration (FHA)	A federal agency that insures first mortgages; it enables buyers to make a smaller down payment.
Federal National Mortgage Association	*See* Fannie Mae.
fee simple*	In modern estates, the terms "fee" and "fee simple" are substantially synonymous. The term establishes the title of real property in the owner, without limitation or end. The owner may dispose of it by sale, or trade or will.
first-line underwriter	The underwriter at a lending institution that has first signature authority on a loan. Depending on the size of the loan, the first-line underwriter may be able to give an approval.
fixed balloon note	A fixed balloon note has a low rate for a period of time that rolls into a no-option, or deadend, situation. You must pay off the loan at the point the balloon is due.
fixed interim-rate mortgage (FIRM)	Two types are possible: (1) low start, fixed for five or seven years, with a one-time adjustment to another fixed rate for the life of the loan, or (2) low start, fixed for three, five, seven, or ten years, that rolls into an adjustable-rate mortgage with interest or payment caps for the duration. *See also* two-step mortgage.
fixed-rate mortgage	A fixed-rate mortgage means a steady, flat payment of principal and interest, with no rate change throughout the life of the loan.

four Cs	Capacity, Credit, Collateral and Character —the four criteria by which your eligibility for a home loan are judged.
Freddie Mac (Federal Home Loan Mortgage Corporation)	A federally chartered, but shareholder-owned, company, similar to Fannie Mae; a quasi-governmental agency.
full documentation	A type of loan package that includes everything relevant. Everything on the application is verified.
fully amortizing	Repayment schedule of your loan over a specific time with equal payments, principal plus interest; the result of a zero balance.
fully indexed	Describes the interest rate of an adjustable rate mortgage; index plus the margin equals the fully indexed interest rate. The index is subject to change with the economy, and the margin is fixed for the life of the loan.
functional obsolescence	A feature of the property that reduces its market value, for example, a house with one bathroom but four bedrooms in a family neighborhood where comparable properties have two bathrooms.
funding	The day the borrower and the lender put all the money in escrow.
garbage fees	Fees assessed as part of non-recurring closing costs that are aggravating and/or ridiculous.
gift	A portion of your down payment given by a relative. There are cautions associated with a gift: Lenders want borrowers to contribute at least 5 percent of the purchase price from their own funds. This

	minimum contribution must be used as down payment.
gift letter	A gift letter must clearly state there is no expectation of repayment, and precisely what the giver's relationship is to the recipient. (The donor must also prove the ability to "gift the funds.")
grant deed	This states that title to the property is moving from one person(s) to another.
homeowners association (HOA)	An association of people with common property interests; in the case of condos or planned developments, it's formed by the builder and required by statute in some states. The association is governed by CC and Rs.
homeowners dues	An assessment, usually monthly, that members of a homeowners association must pay for the upkeep of the property in which they have a common interest.
HUD-1	Final closing statement from title company showing all fees paid. It is divided into two parts, a credit side and a debit side, balancing to zero.
HUP	Slang for "Hurry Up" credit report, an abridged version of a full credit report required with the loan application.
impounds*	A trust-type account established by lenders for the accumulation of funds to meet taxes, FHA mortgage insurance premiums, and/or future insurance policy premiums required to protect their security. Impounds are usually collected with the note payment.

income approach*	One of the three methods in the appraisal process; an analysis in which the estimated gross income from the subject residence is used as a basis for estimating value along with gross rent multipliers derived.
index	Used to establish rate changes for an adjustable rate mortgage; it moves with the economy.
inquiries	A record on your credit report that someone has requested credit information about you. Be sure you gave that company or individual permission to request it.
installment debt	You pay the same amount every month for the life of the loan, for example, a car loan.
institutional lenders	Lenders such as inter- and intra-state banks, certain securities firms, savings and loans (including thrifts), credit unions, and some mortgage bankers.
interest rate*	The percentage of a sum of money charged for its use.
introductory rate	A lower-than-usual rate designed to entice a borrower; a start-rate that is less than the fully indexed rate.
joint tenancy*	Joint ownership by two or more persons with right of survivorship; all joint tenants own equal interest and have equal rights in the property.
jumbo	A loan size exceeding $207,000.
judgment	A decision in the courts, at whatever level, determining that someone owes someone money. If it appears on your credit report,

	it's a legal decision stating that you owe someone money, or that you owed it and paid it to "satisfy the judgment."
leasehold estate*	A tenant's right to occupy real estate during the term of the lease. This is a personal property interest.
lien*	A form of encumbrance that usually makes property security for the payment of a debt or discharge of an obligation, for example, a tax lien.
limited documentation	A type of loan application package documenting your borrowing status through the normal sources. It is an accommodation to the borrower in the sense that you have alternatives in the way you satisfy the underwriting requirements to secure the loan as fast as possible.
liquid assets	Cash and investments you can immediately turn into cash.
loan application*	The loan application (also known as the 1003) is a source of information on which the lender decides to make the loan, defines the terms of the loan contract; gives the name of the borrower, place of employment, salary, bank accounts, and credit references; and, describes the real estate that is to be mortgaged. It also stipulates the amount of loan being applied for and repayment terms.
loan processor	Ensures that the proper documents are in the borrower's file.
loan-to-value ratio (LTV)	With a 20 percent down payment, the loan amount is 80 percent of the value of the property, so the LTV is 80 percent, that is, the percentage of a property's

value that a lender can or may loan to a borrower.

locked   Confirmed and committed to, as in, "the rate is locked."

locking in   *See* locked.

margin   A constant used to calculate the rate of an adjustable rate mortgage. While the index changes, the margin added to it to determine the rate stays constant.

marking to market   Making a loan that stays close to the cost of funds for a bank, i.e., an adjustable rate loan.

mechanics lien   A lien placed by a contractor or building supply source for a bill not paid as agreed.

mortgage*   An instrument recognized by law by which property is hypothecated to secure the payment of a debt or obligation; procedure for foreclosure in event of default is established by statute.

mortgage banker   A conduit to funds from a lender that normally does not take deposits and funds loans off lines of credit.

mortgage broker   represents property buyer or owner to lender to obtain a mortgage or refinance. Services include prequalification, loan selection, packaging the application to match underwriting criteria, and guiding the mortgage from origination to closing.

mortgage insurance
(MI, PMI, private
mortgage insurance)   Generally required if you make a down payment less than 20 percent. It is designed to protect the lender against default. You can estimate it at .53 percent of the loan amount per year. (Example: $100,000 × .0053)

negatively amortizing	Creation of principal by making less-than-interest-only payments; a loan that offers negative amortization gives the borrower the maximum amount of control.
no income stated	A type of loan application package, primarily for the self-employed borrower, that involves no tax returns or specific verification of income. A no-income stated package means that you build a case for your capacity without telling the lender how much you make. Ratios are not calculated; your credit must be perfect and your reserves strong.
non-institutional lenders	Non-depository lenders such as mortgage bankers, pension funds, and private lenders.
paid as agreed	Describes an account for which payments are made precisely as specified by the creditor. An important criterion in determining creditworthiness.
personal property*	Any property that is not real property.
PITI	Principal, Interest, Taxes and Insurance. This acronym, or PI (Principal and Interest), is often used to mean "the whole monthly loan payment."
point	One percent of the loan amount, paid up front as part of the closing costs, to reduce the rate of interest on the loan.
pool	A group of loans with the same characteristics.
pool underwriter	Third-party with no relationship to the pool or investment who certifies that ample evidence exists that the loan contains all

the characteristics that make it worthy of pool insurance, meaning that it is securitizable.

portfolio loan	A special deal made by a lender to accommodate a preferred customer; usually made with no expectation of sale into the secondary market.
preliminary title report	A report showing the condition of the title before the sale.
premium	Increased interest rate or extra points paid for a certain type loan (such as a quick qualifier which requires more lender faith) or your less than desirable qualifications (such as a bad credit report).
prepaid items	Includes items paid out of pocket, like appraisal and credit report fees.
prepayment penalty * (PPP)	Penalty for the payment of a mortgage or trust deed note before it actually becomes due if the note does not provide for payment.
prequalification	An analysis of your income and debt to determine borrowing power.
primary market	The mortgage origination source.
private mortgage insurance (PMI)	*See* mortgage insurance.
qualifying ratios	Ratios expressing the relationship of income to debt, including a particular home loan, that provide a benchmark about your ability to handle monthly payments on the home loan.
quick qualifier (QQ)	With the quick qualifier as with the no-income stated, normally no verification of income is required. You need alternative

	documentation of assets and payment history; ratios have to be right and your credit perfect.
quitclaim deed*	A deed to relinquish any interest in property that the grantor may have.
refinancing*	The paying off of an existing obligation and assuming a new obligation in its place.
Residential Loan Application	The standard mortgage application, also known as form 1003 (Fannie Mae) and form 65 (Freddie Mac).
RESPA	Real Estate Settlement Procedures Act.
return on assets (ROA)	The amount of money an institution makes on its overall holdings.
revolving debt	You are required to pay a portion of the balance each month, for example, most credit cards.
rolling late	The same delinquency that appears in more than one late column. The problem can arise and persist when you are 30 days late with a January payment, for instance, then make a payment in February that is automatically credited to February. When you make a payment in March, your January payment is still considered delinquent and it would "roll over" into the 60-day category.
seasoned funds	Funds that have been in your account for at least 60 to 90 days.
second job	For purposes of including income from a second job as part of your qualifying income, you must be able to document that it is continuing employment, not just a short-term exercise to improve your

cash flow this month. A less objective criterion is that the second job should have a relationship to the first, although that is not as important as the probability of the job continuing.

secondary market   The market into which mortgages are sold by the originating source, or sold from one institution to another within the market.

securitized   A way of saying "insured" that refers to a mortgage. A loan that is securitized, or securitizable, meets certain criteria that make it sellable in the secondary market.

self-qualification   A self-assessment of your income and debt to determine borrowing power.

selling a mortgage   The lender gets the amount of the loan, but transfers the risk and interest-earning potential to another lender.

service a loan   Handle the ongoing administative aspects of a loan.

spot index   Basis for ARM adjustment involving a preset formula applied at a "spot in time" that affects your rate for an extended period thereafter. For example, the formula might be that 45 days before your annual adjustment date, the one-year U.S. Treasury rate on that particular day (plus the margin) dictates your rate for the next year.

super jumbo   A loan size generally more than $650,000.

sweat equity   Slang meaning that ownership in property that was enhanced by the investment of labor to improve it, hence increase its value.

teaser rate	*See* introductory rate.
title insurance*	Insurance written by a title company to protect property owner against loss if title is imperfect.
title report*	A report that discloses condition of the title, made by a title company preliminary to issuance of title insurance.
top ratio	The percentage of your gross monthly income that the lender will allow for monthly housing costs.
total purchase cost	This amount is composed of the earnest money deposit, down payment, and total due at closing.
trailing spouse income	If a two-income couple has temporarily become a one-income couple because of a relocation related to career advancement, in calculating ratios, the lender would use a combination of the relocated spouse's current income plus the "trailing spouse's" most recent income.
two-step mortgage	Two types are possible: (1) low start, fixed for five or seven years, with a one-time adjustment to another fixed rate for the life of the loan; or (2) low start, fixed for three, five, seven, or ten years, that rolls into an adjustable-rate mortgage with interest or payment caps for the duration. *See also* fixed interim-rate mortgage.
underwriting*	The technical analysis by a lender to determine the borrower's ability to repay a contemplated loan.
verification of deposit	A document from your bank that verifies the amounts deposited into the account in a given period.

verification of mortgage	A document from your mortgage holder that verifies that you make payments as agreed.
verification of rent	A document from your landlord that verifies that you make payments as agreed.
Veterans Administration (VA)	Applicable only to veterans of United States military service, the VA loan has a current limit of around $200,000, but that amount is increased periodically.
weighted average coupon (WAC)	Average interest rate of loans that are grouped together and sold to the secondary market.
weighted average maturity (WAM)	Average number of months remaining on loans that are grouped together and sold to the secondary market.
weighted index	Basis for an ARM adjustment; the index's movement with the economy on a monthly basis affects your interest rate and payment size on a monthly basis, for example, the 11th District Cost of Funds Index.

Appendix A

Directory of Mortgage-Related Web Sites

The following World Wide Web sites are a sampling of those that help meet mortgage-related needs, from online mortgage services to in-depth information about specific topics.

Mortgage Services:

AAA National Mortgage Directory	www.dirs.com/mortgage/
Countryside Mortgage Services	www.cais.net/countryside
Homebuyer's Fair	www.homefair.com
Homes & Land	homes.com/
HSH Associates Financial Publishers	www.hsh.com
Mortgage Maze	www.maze.com

Consumer Information:

Consumer Mortgage Information Network	www.human.com/proactive/index.html
Fannie Mae	www.fanniemae.com
Freddie Mac	www.freddiemac.com
The Guide to Real Estate on the Internet	www.travelersonline.com/guide
National Association of Home Builders	www.nahb.com
The PMI Group, Inc.	/www.pmigroup.com/consumer/

Appendix B

Sample One

*Your Name**
111 Your Street
Your Town, Your State 11111

Credit Agency
111 The Address
The Town, The State 11111

January 1, 1997

To Whom It May Concern:

This letter is a formal complaint that you are reporting inaccurate credit information.

I am very upset that you have included the information mentioned below in my credit profile and have not maintained reasonable procedures in your operations to assure complete accuracy in the credit reports published by your bureau.

The Fair Credit Reporting Act of 1971 ensures that bureaus report only 100% accurate credit information. Every step must be taken to assure the information reported is correct and accurate in it's entirety.

The following information, accordingly, needs to be verified and deleted from the report as soon as possible:

Creditor's name, account # 9876-54321-xyz

The above item should not be included in my report as my account because it is not mine (this is the reason the report is in error). This is an error in reporting. Please delete this information,

* Complete the italicized type with your personal information.

and supply a corrected credit profile to all creditors who have received a copy of the inaccurate information within the last 6 months, or the last 2 years for employment purposes.

Also, please provide me with the name, address, and telephone number for each credit grantor or other subscriber.

Sincerely,

Your Signature

Sample Two

Your Name*
111 Your Street
Your Town, Your State 11111
Credit Agency
111 The Address
The Town, The State 11111
January 31, 1997

Regarding: *Dispute Letter Dated January 1, 1997*

To Whom It May Concern:

This letter is formal notice that you have failed to respond in a timely manner to my dispute letter dated *January 1, 1997*. Based on the Return-Receipt which has been delivered by the Post Office, you received my letter.

As you are well aware, federal law requires you to respond within a reasonable period of time, and I have given you over 30 days to do so, yet you have failed to respond. Failure to comply with these federal regulations by credit reporting agencies are investigated by the Federal Trade Commission (see 15 USC 41, et seq.). I am maintaining a careful record of my communications with your agency on this matter, for the purpose of filing a complaint with the FTC should you continue in your non-compliance.

Be aware that I am making a final goodwill attempt to have you clear up this matter. You have 15 days to make amends.

For your benefit, and as a gesture of my goodwill, I will restate my original dispute. The following information needs to be verified and deleted from my credit report as soon as possible:

Creditor's name, account # 9876-54321-xyz

The listed item is completely incorrect and has been reported in error. Please delete this misleading information, and supply a corrected credit profile to all creditors who have received a copy within the last 6 months, or the last 2 years for employment purposes.

Additionally, please provide the name, address, and telephone number for each credit grantor or other subscriber.

Sincerely,

Your Signature
Your Name
Your Social Security Number

* **Complete the italicized type with your personal information.**

Index